VISUAL QUICKSTART GUIDE

Kai's Power Tools 3

FOR MACINTOSH

Sandee Cohen

Peachpit Press

Visual QuickStart Guide
Kai's Power Tools 3 for Macintosh
Sandee Cohen

Peachpit Press

2414 Sixth Street
Berkeley, CA 94710
510/548-4393
510/548-5991 (fax)
800/283-9444

Find us on the World Wide Web at:
http://www.peachpit.com
Peachpit Press is a division of Addison Wesley Longman

Copyeditor: Karen Dominey
Cover design: The Visual Group
Production: Sandee Cohen
Index: Steve Rath

This book was created using: QuarkXPress 3.3 for layout; Adobe Photoshop 4 running Kai's Power Tools 3, KPT Convolver, and KPT Actions for illustrations; and Ambrosia SW Snapz Pro for screen shots. The computer used was a Macintosh PowerPC™ 8500 and a Duo 2300. The fonts used were Minion, Futura Condensed Extra Bold, and Zapf Dingbats from Adobe. All photographs were taken from the KPT PowerPhotos and MetaPhotos collections.

Notice of Rights

Notice of Liability

Trademarks

ISBN 0-201-68816-6

9 8 7 6 5 4 3 2 1

Printed and bound in the United States of America

DEDICATED TO

All my students—past, present, and future—who teach me what makes a program easy to learn, and what needs a book to explain it all.

Dad, Terry, Bonnie, Jeffry, Dan, Liz, and Sarah, who don't do graphics, but still read my books.

THANKS TO

Ted Nace, of Peachpit Press, who started this ball rolling.

Victor Gavenda, my project editor at Peachpit Press, who helped focus and fine-tune the book. Victor came into this project knowing more about Kai's Power Tools than any editor should!

Kate Reber, of Peachpit Press who was a terrific source of production as well as design advice!

Nancy Ruenzel, and the rest of the Peachpit gang.

Karen Dominey, a terrific copyeditor, who really worked with me on this one.

Steve Rath, who came through with time to do the index. I don't think I want to do any books without an index by Steve.

Sharon Steuer, Author of the *Illustrator Wow Book,* who told me she'd start using KPT 3 if I wrote a VQS explaining it. OK Sharon, here it is!

Pixel for making sure the pages printed correctly.

Ted Alspach After you've learned the basics of KPT 3 here, check out his *Kai's Power Tools Studio Secrets.*

Jen Alspach, who knows FreeHand! And likes to exchange tips and tricks about it.

John Wilczak of MetaTools for his kind words of encouragement.

Holly Fisher, formerly at MetaTools, who helped me get everything I needed.

Teresa Bridwell and Sally Olmstead of MetaTools who kept me right on top of the latest info.

Greg Quinn of MetaTools who patiently explained the stuff I couldn't understand.

John Feld of MetaTools who also believes in the power of KPT Convolver (and told me how to cheat to get the stars).

Sree Kotay for being so helpful.

TABLE OF CONTENTS

Chapter 1 **Background Stuff** **1**
In the beginning 1
Why all the interest? 2
Why a Kai's Power Tools book? 2
What's in the book? 3
How to use this book 4
About the art 5

Chapter 2 **Installation** **7**
Installing Kai's Power Tools 8
Installing using an alias 9
System requirements 10
Allocating more RAM 10
Installing the electronic manual 11
Installing Kai's Classic Power Tips 11
Installing the KPT 2.1 and bonus filters 12

Chapter 3 **Interface** **13**
Spheroid Designer 14
Gradient Designer 17
Texture Explorer 20
Interform 23
Compact Filters 26
Lens f/x 28
Common elements 29

Chapter 4 **Spheroid Designer** **31**
Preparing to make a plain sphere 32
Clearing the settings 33
Coloring a plain sphere 34
Changing the direction of the light 35
Creating a matte surface 36
Creating a shiny surface 36
Creating more colors in a sphere 37
Working with the Memory Dots 38
Using the Add Preset button 38
Using the Preset menu 39
Adding a bump map to a sphere 40
Adjusting the bump map 41
Adjusting the Sphere Curvature 42
Adjusting the transparency of a sphere 43

Creating multiple spheres
in a random pattern 44
Using the Mutation Tree. 45

Chapter 5   **Gradient Designer** **47**
Preparing to make a gradient 48
Clearing the Gradient Designer settings . . . 49
Choosing colors for a gradient 50
Changing the direction and loop
of a gradient 50
Increasing the repetitions 51
Working with the Gradient Bracket 52
Selecting a shade of gray. 53
Selecting a transparency. 53
Using the Opacity Control panel. 54
Creating circular and elliptical sunbursts . . . 55
Creating square and rectangular bursts 56
Creating a radial sweep 56
Changing the center of the gradient 57
Creating angular and circular shapebursts . . 57
Creating angular and circular pathbursts . . . 58
Using the Gradients on Paths. 58
Creating a Grayscale Mapburst. 59
Adjust the Loop controls 60
Adjusting the Gradient Modifiers 61
Using the Add Preset button 62
Using the Preset menu. 62
Using the Swap RGB presets 63
Using the Swap Alpha presets. 63

Chapter 6   **Texture Explorer** **65**
Preparing to make a texture. 65
Changing the Source Texture 66
Controlling the mutations 66
Setting the Mutation Options 67
Using the Color Globe. 67
Using the Gradient Bar 68
Moving the Source Texture 68
Changing the texture size 69
Changing the texture direction. 69
Using the Opacity Control panel. 70
Adjusting the Gradient Modifiers 71
Setting Texture Protection 72
Using the Add Preset button 72
Using the Preset menu. 73

Chapter 7   **Interform** **75**

Static Images 76
Preparing to create an Interform texture . . . 76
Turning off the motion options 76
Creating an Offspring texture 77
Changing the Influence of the
Parent textures 77
Working with the Frame panels 78
Using the Add Preset button 78
Using the Preset menu 79
Using the Opacity Control panel 79
Animated Images 80
Adding Manual Scooting 80
Using the UniMotion options 81
Changing the UniMotion speed 81
Manual Blending 82
Adding UniMotion Blending 83
Filling the Frame panels 83
Setting the Movie options 84
Recording a movie 85

Chapter 8   **Compact Filters** **87**

Glass Lens 88
Making a selection for the Glass Lens 88
Creating a Glass Lens 89
Page Curl 90
Creating a Page Curl 90
Creating a transparent Page Curl 91
Planar Tile 92
Seamless Welder 93
Twirl 94
Using the Twirl mode 94
Using the Kaleidoscope mode 94
Video Feedback 95
Vortex Tile 96
3D Stereo Noise 97

Chapter 9   **Lens f/x Filters** **99**

Pixel f/x 100
Gaussian f/x 101
Edge f/x 102
Intensity f/x 103
Smudge f/x 104
Noise f/x 105
MetaToys f/x 106
Using the Glass Lens f/x filter 106
Using the Twirl f/x filter 107

Table of Contents

Chapter 10   Texture Explorer 2.1 . . . . **109**
    Preparing to make a texture 110
    Changing the Source Texture 110
    Using the Preview window 110
    Controlling the mutations 110
    Using the Shuffle button 111
    Using the Color Globe 111
    Using the Gradient Bar 112
    Moving the Source Texture 112
    Using the Transparency Option 113
    Applying a Global Transparency 113
    Selecting the Tile Size 114
    Using Texture Protection 114
    Using the Add Preset button 115
    Using the Preset menu 115
    Using the Preset Keyboard Shortcuts 115

Chapter 11   Fractal Explorer **117**
    Understanding fractals 118
    Preparing to make a fractal design 118
    Clearing the Fractal Explorer 119
    The six fractal shapes 120
    Moving around a shape 121
    Zooming in and out of a design 122
    Using the Zoom slider 122
    Clearing the Gradient Wrapping panel . . . 123
    Changing the outside color 123
    Changing the Loop order 124
    Changing the inside color 124
    Using the Wrapping Controls 125
    Using the Opacity Control panel 126
    Using the Shuffle button 127
    Using the Detail Control 128
    Storing fractal designs 129
    Using the Preset menu 129

Chapter 12   Apply Modes **131**
    Locating the Apply modes 131
    Normal 132
    Procedural + ... 132
    Procedural - 132
    Darken Only 133
    Lighten Only 133
    Multiply 133
    Screen 134

	Difference	134
	Add	134
	Subtract	135
Chapter 13	**Convolver**	**137**
	Installing Convolver	137
	Interface	138
	Mode buttons	139
	Grid/Preview Diamond	139
	Current Tile	139
	Explore controls	140
	Axis arrows	140
	Effect names	140
	Effect menu	140
	Effect marbles	141
	Opening Convolver	141
	Tweak Linear Convolution Mode	141
	Clearing the Tweak mode settings	141
	Using Blur/Sharpen	142
	Using Edges Amount/Edges Angle	142
	Using Relief Amount/Relief Angle	143
	Using Hue Rotate	143
	Using Saturation	143
	Using Brightness	143
	Using Tint	144
	Using Fade to Grey	144
	Using Color Control	144
	Reset to Normal	144
	Effect Intensity	144
	Tweak Unsharp/Gaussian Mode	144
	Using Gaussian and Radius	145
	Using Unsharp, Radius and Threshold	145
	Tweak Difference Mask Mode	146
	Design Mode	146
	Explore Mode	147
	Split Screen Preview	148
	Change View area	148
	Using Memory Dots	149
	Presets menu	149
	Options	150
	Convolver Preferences	150
	Earning Stars	151
Chapter 14	**MetaPhotos**	**153**
	Choosing HiRes or LoRes files	154
	Changing HiRes file sizes	154
	Alpha Channels	156

Table of Contents

Using Alpha Channels to create
  composite images 156
Using Alpha Channels to create a
  drop shadow 157
Using Alpha Channels to create a glow . . . 158
Using Transflectance Channels 159
Creating a path 160
Creating a Clipping path. 160

Chapter 15   **KPT Actions** **161**
Requirements 161
Installing KPT Actions 162
Adding the KPT Actions presets 162
Running Actions in Photoshop 163
Running Text actions. 164
Running Frame actions 164
Running Buttons and
  Backgrounds actions 165
Recording a Simple action. 166
Modifying an Existing action 168

Index **171**

BACKGROUND STUFF

Welcome to the world of Kai's Power Tools and other KPT products such as Convolver, MetaPhotos, and KPT Actions. It's hard to conceive of any other series of products that has generated as much excitement among software users.

In the beginning...

Kai's Power Tools started with the genius of Kai (pronounced Kye) Krause. He recognized there was a software program, Adobe Photoshop, that offered users enormous power in its channels and filters. Yet most people were hardly taking advantage of all that Photoshop could do. Kai started out with a series of simple files that showed how to use the channels of Photoshop to create fascinating effects. These tips, called Kai's Power Tips, were distributed via electronic bulletin boards. Within a short time Kai's fame had spread as one of the premiere experts on Photoshop.

Later on, Kai realized the potential of the filter technology that Adobe had created for Photoshop. Instead of trying to make a version of Photoshop that could do everything, Adobe let outside companies create filters that would plug into Photoshop to make different effects. Finally, in 1992, Kai Krause joined in a partnership with John Wilczak to create the first version of Kai's Power Tools. Instead of simple filters that could only blur or add noise to existing images, Kai's Power Tools provided entire new sets of features to create new objects.

At the time it seemed rather strange to create a product that was limited to running only through someone else's program. But, five years later, with hundreds of thousands of copies of Kai's Power Tools 3 sold, the wisdom of the venture is obvious.

Why all the interest?

What has made Kai's Power Tools one of the most successful set of third-party filters? Well, the first reason must be how much the software can do. For instance, in the years when Photoshop could only create two-color linear or radial gradients, the KPT Gradient Designer was mixing multi-colors in linear, radial, shape, burst, and other types of gradients.

Or, when Photoshop was limited to creating textures of noise, the KPT Texture Explorer could create unlimited textures ranging from earth, wood, metals, water, and outer space effects. Or when Photoshop could hardly do more than pinch images or create a fish-eye look to them, the KPT Spheroid Designer was creating spheres, balls, marbles, and all sorts of other images.

It's hard to find an area of advertising, design, graphics, or publishing that does not use a version of Kai's Power Tools. Just look through a magazine and you'll see page curls, glows, twirls, tiles, and textures—all of which could only come from a set of Kai's Power Tools.

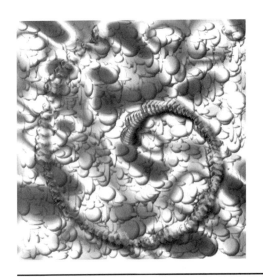

Why a Kai's Power Tools book?

Just as there are manuals and other books to give you tips and tricks for working with programs such as Photoshop, the time has come for a manual to help

explain the depth of Kai's Power Tools. While there are many who have been able to jump right into the unique KPT interface and start creating immediately, there are many others who have found the interface confusing. They are more comfortable with a clean, no-frills interface. It is for those no-nonsense types that this book was created.

What's in the book?

Just as Kai's Power Tools broke all the rules for software design and features, so does this book break many of the rules in the Peachpit Press *Visual QuickStart* series. First, the book covers not just one software program. Rather than limit the book to just Kai's Power Tools, it covers several other MetaTools products.

Chapters 2 through 12 provide a comprehensive tour of Kai's Power Tools 3, as well as two filters from Kai's Power Tools 2.1. The early chapters start with installing the filters and understanding the Interface. Then, each of the separate filters is covered in its own chapter. A special chapter on the Apply Modes covers how all the filters can be made to interact with existing images.

Next, the book looks at Convolver— one of the most underrated, unappreciated third-party filters from MetaTools. Convolver is a separate program from Kai's Power Tools and, if you don't have it, you should take a look at this chapter. You may discover that Convolver is the answer to many of your design and production needs.

Next, the book covers working with the set of stock photos published by MetaTools under the name MetaPhotos. Of course, the term stock photos hardly does justice to these images. Unlike many other photo collections with plain, dull, and ordinary images, the MetaPhotos collections are unique in both their composition and their production.

You may be wondering, though, how much there is to working with a scanned photo. Well, when you look through the chapter, you will see it contains exercises that explain some of the ways you can work with the alpha channels, paths, and special transflectance channels that are included with the images. In fact, even if you never open a single MetaPhotos image, you will still use many of the techniques in that chapter for working with other images.

Finally, the book covers one of the newest products from MetaTools, KPT Actions. This is an accessory kit that enhances Kai's Power Tools 3 when working with Photoshop 4. Talk about a specialty market! But as soon as you see what KPT Actions lets you do, you'll want to have it installed for your copy of Kai's Power Tools.

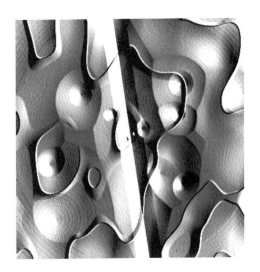

How to use this book

Most of the chapters in the book are totally self-contained. That means that if you're interested mostly in the KPT Texture Explorer, you can skip immediately to that chapter. The only chapters you should look at first are Chapter 2, "Installation," and Chapter 3, "Interface." This will make sure your copy of Kai's Power Tools is installed correctly and that you understand the general conventions of the filters.

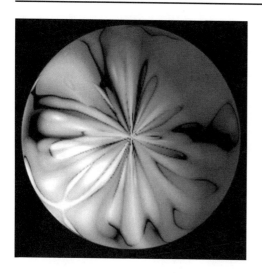

About the art

Most of the chapters in this book have opening artwork that was created using the KPT filters or the KPT product discussed in that chapter. With the exception of the chapter on MetaPhotos that used images from the MetaPhotos collections, all the artwork started with totally blank files. The images came solely from using the filters mentioned in the chapter. No other images or filters were allowed. (This wasn't a limitation from the filters—just a little challenge for me.) As you can see from the artwork, even with that limitation, I was able to create some extremely interesting artwork.

I thoroughly expect that with this book, you too will be creating similar artwork—if not even better. Good luck! And don't forget to have fun!

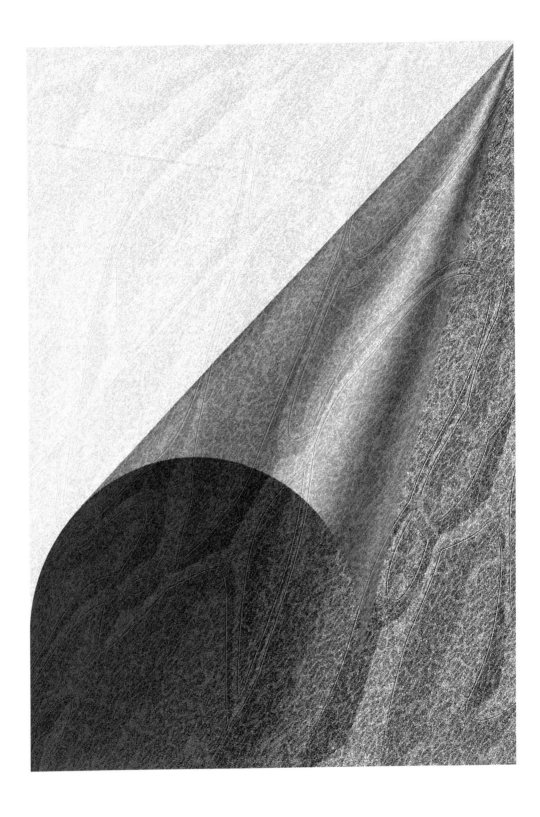

INSTALLATION 2

B efore you can use Kai's Power Tools, you will need to install it. This is different from installing most other software applications. When you install a typical program, that is all you need. However, when you install Kai's Power Tools, it needs another program, called a host application. And how you install Kai's Power Tools depends on where your host application is located.

In this chapter you will learn

◆ Installing Kai's Power Tools in the proper folder for your host application.

◆ Installing the filters in more than one host application.

◆ The system requirements for the filters.

◆ Increasing the memory allotted to the host application.

◆ Installing the KPT 3 electronic manual.

◆ Installing the Kai's classic power tips.

Figure 1. *A host application such as Adobe Photoshop* is needed to run Kai's Power Tools.

A host application (**Figure 1**) is the application within which you will be running Kai's Power Tools. Any application that supports Photoshop-compatible plug-ins can be a host application for Kai's Power Tools. Obviously this includes Adobe Photoshop. It also includes other imaging programs such as Fractal Design Painter. Other programs such as Adobe Illustrator, Macromedia FreeHand, and Macromedia Director will support some, but not all, of Kai's Power Tools.

After you have your host application installed you can then install Kai's Power Tools.

Installing Kai's Power Tools

1. Insert the CD that came with Kai's Power Tools. The disk should open automatically to reveal the main window (**Figure 2**).

2. Double-click the icon labeled KPT 3 Install.1. A dialog box with important information about Kai's Power Tools will appear. You can read the message onscreen, print it, or save it to your hard drive. Click the Continue button to continue with the installation process.

3. The installer program will ask you to select your Adobe Photoshop Plug-ins folder. This folder does not have to be a component of Photoshop but can belong to any application that accepts Photoshop plug-ins.

4. Once you have found the host application's plug-ins folder, use the Select button to select it. The name of the folder you selected will then appear in the installation window (**Figure 3**).

5. Click the Install button to start the installation process.

6. After all the files have been installed, you can quit the installer.

7. When the host application is running, you will be able to access the Kai's Power Tools through the Filter menu of the host application.

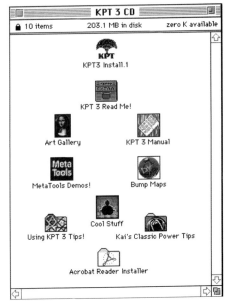

Figure 2. *The main window that opens when you insert the* ***KPT 3 CD***.

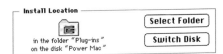

Figure 3. *When you have selected the* ***plug-ins folder*** *for the* ***host application***, *its name will appear in the installation window.*

Figure 4. *The KPT 3 filters can be installed inside their own folder within the Photoshop plug-ins folder.*

Figure 5. *Choose **Make Alias** from the **File** menu to create an alias of the folder containing the KPT 3 filters.*

Tips

◆ Instead of putting all your KPT 3 filters loosely in your plug-ins folder, you may want to put them in a folder of their own (**Figure 4**). Do not move any of the KPT 3 filters to sub-folders or they will not work properly.

◆ As soon as you quit the installer, a registration form will appear. You can fill this out electronically and send it, via modem, to MetaTools. You can also print the registration form and fax or mail it to the address on the printout.

If you have more than one application that can use Kai's Power Tools, you can use aliases to install it into others.

Installing Kai's Power Tools using an alias

1. Select the folder that contains the filters. This can be the folder for just the KPT 3 filters or the plug-ins folder that holds all your Adobe Photoshop plug-ins.

2. From the File menu, choose Make Alias (**Figure 5**).

3. Place the alias folder into the proper plug-ins folder for the additional host applications.

4. When the host application is running, you will then be able to access the Kai's Power Tools through the Filter menu of the host application.

Tips

◆ Many host applications let you designate a plug-ins folder by using the program's Preferences setting.

Installing using an Alias

System requirements

The following are the hardware configurations for Kai's Power Tools.

◆ Power Macintosh or Quadra Macintosh with a floating point unit.

◆ System 7.1 or higher.

◆ Any image editing application that 100% supports the Adobe standard plug-in architecture.

◆ 2.5 MB RAM from the host program's memory allocation.

◆ Recommended: a color monitor with a 24-bit video card or enough VRAM to display "millions" of colors.

Tip

◆ While it is possible to run Kai's Power Tools on a Macintosh Quadra, some filters, especially Interform, will run their best on a Power Macintosh.

Because Kai's Power Tools are so powerful you may need to increase the memory for the host application.

Allocating more RAM to the host application

1. With the host application not running, select its icon.

2. Choose Get Info (Command-I) from the File menu. The Get Info window will appear (**Figure 6**).

3. Increase the preferred size amount. Close the window. Restart the host application.

4. If you still experience difficulty, quit the application and then repeat steps 1, 2, and 3.

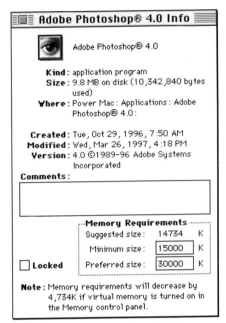

Figure 6. *The **Get Info** window of the host application allows you to increase the memory allocated to the application.*

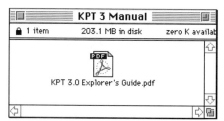

Figure 7. *The **PDF version** of the manual can be copied from the CD onto your hard disk for reference.*

Kai's Power Tools comes with a printed manual called the Explorer's Guide. However, you should also install the electronic version that is on the CD. This is a PDF document which contains information that was not included in the printed manual.

Installing the KPT 3 electronic manual

1. Open the KPT 3 CD and find the icon labeled KPT 3 Manual (**Figure 7**).

2. Open that icon and copy the document labeled KPT 3.0 Explorer's Guide.pdf onto your hard disk.

3. If you already have the Acrobat Reader 2.1 or later installed on your hard disk, you can then open the Explorer Guide.

4. If you do not have the Acrobat Reader, open the folder labeled Acrobat Reader Installer and double-click on the Acrobat Reader 2.1 Install.

5. Follow the Installer directions as to how to install the Reader. After the Reader is installed, you can open the Explorer Guide.

Figure 8. *The **Classic Power Tips** folder contains tips and tricks for working with Adobe Photoshop.*

If you are working with Adobe Photoshop as the host application, you may be interested in Kai's Classic Power Tips. This is a series of documents containing special techniques for getting the most from Photoshop.

Installing Kai's Classic Power Tips

1. Drag the folder labeled Kai's Classic Power Tips onto your hard drive (**Figure 8**).

2. Open the folder and double-click on the icon labeled Kai's Power Tips.

3. The other items in the Kai's Classic Power Tips folder are support files for use in working with the tips.

Installing the electronic manual;
Installing Kai's Classic Power Tips

Kai's Power Tools is currently at version 3 and there have been many improvements over version 2.0. Ordinarily, that would mean that you would not want any previous versions of Kai's Power Tools.

However, two filters, Texture Explorer 2.1 and Fractal Explorer 2.1, offered features that have been dropped from version 3. So in addition to version 3, you can install the 2.1 version of the Texture Explorer and Fractal Explorer. Finally, as an added bonus, the original Selection Info and Cyclone filters have also been included.

Installing the KPT 2.1 and bonus filters

1. Open the KPT 3 CD and open the folder Cool Stuff.

2. Open the folder labeled TE & FE Classic.

3. If you have a Power Macintosh, drag the KPT 2.1 Filters PPC folder (**Figure 9**) into the plug-ins folder for your host application. If you have a Macintosh Quadra, drag the KPT 2.1 Filters 68K folder.

Once you have finished installing Kai's Power Tools, you can open your host application in the usual fashion. Kai's Power Tools will appear under the application's filter menu. You are now ready to work with Kai's Power Tools.

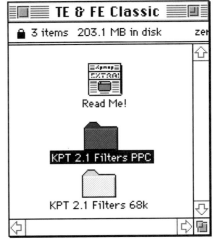

Figure 9. *Drag the **KPT 2.1 Filters PPC folder** into your plug-ins folder to access the bonus filters.*

INTERFACE 3

When you launch Kai's Power Tools, you are actually entering a whole new world of computer controls. This is the famous user interface that was designed by Kai Krause.

The interface was designed "to make things friendly and fairly intuitive, without insulting your intelligence or including eyesores for labels." The purpose was to let you explore, play, and wander through the filters as you might if given a huge box of special effects. However, that kind of exploration takes time—time you might not have. That is why this chapter explicitly labels and shows you the various controls for each of the filters.

In this chapter you will learn

◆ The KPT Spheroid Designer elements.

◆ The KPT Gradient Designer elements.

◆ The KPT Texture Explorer elements.

◆ The KPT Interform elements.

◆ The Compact Filters elements.

◆ The Lens f/x Filters elements.

◆ The common elements found in all of the KPT 3 filters.

Take a moment to look through this chapter. Then keep it available as you go through the exercises. This way you can easily refer to the controls for each of the filters you are working with.

The Spheroid Designer elements

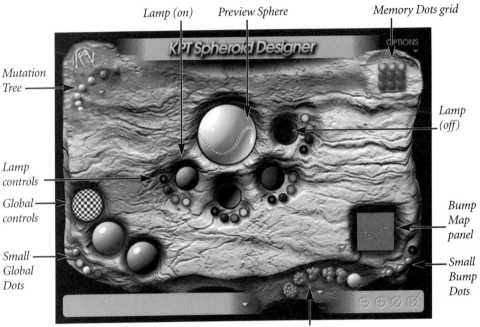

The complete **Spheroid Designer**.

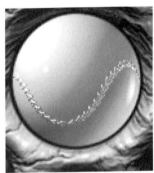

The **Preview Sphere** shows you a small version of the current sphere. Dragging on the sphere also controls the direction of the lighting.

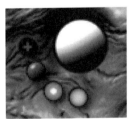

The **Lamps** allow you to turn on and off the lighting. A single click, inside the lamp, will turn the light on or off. Dragging within the lamp will change the direction of the light.

The Spheroid Designer elements

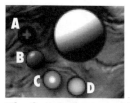

The four **Lamp controls**: Light Polarity (**A**), Light Intensity (**B**), Highlight Intensity (**C**), and Light Hue in RGB (**D**).

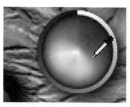

Pressing on the Light Hue in RGB control displays the **Color Picker** which allows you to choose the color of the light.

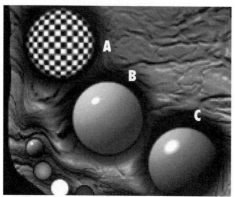

The **Global controls** control the Sphere Curvature (**A**), the Ambient and Gloss Lighting (**B**), and Transparency (**C**).

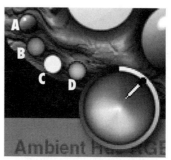

The **Small Global Dots** control the Light Diffusion (**A**), or glossiness of the surface, the Diffuse Hue (**B**), or color of the diffuse light, the Ambient Intensity (**C**), or amount of general light, and the Ambient Hue (**D**), or the color of the general light. Pressing on the Diffuse Hue or the Ambient Hue controls opens the Color Picker.

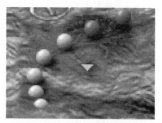

The **Mutation Tree** lets you change the settings in a random manner. Moving your mouse from the bottom to the top of the tree increases the amount of the mutations. Pressing on the white triangle below the tree gives you the options for controlling the mutations.

Spheroid Designer

The Spheroid Designer elements

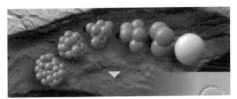

The **Apply Bubbles** allow you to choose from creating one, 10, 50, 100, 500, or 1000 spheres.

Pressing the small white triangle under the Apply Bubbles displays the Apply menu which contains options for how the effects are applied.

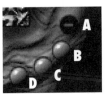

The **Small Bump Dots** allow you to control the Polarity (**A**), or if the surface is raised or indented, the Height (**B**), or the depth of the surface, the Rotation (**C**), or the angle of the surface, and the Zoom (**D**), or how the large the pattern appears on the surface.

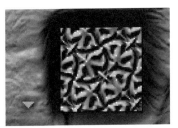

The **Bump Map** panel allows you to see the surface pattern that is being applied to your sphere. Dragging within the panel lets you move the pattern around the surface.

Pressing on the small triangle next to the Bump Map panel displays a Bump Map pop-up menu that allows you to choose from the various surface patterns.

The **Memory Dots** grid is used to store current settings and apply them later.

The Gradient Designer elements

Preview window

Control panels

Control panels

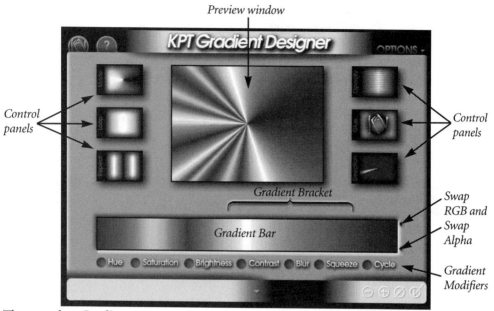

Gradient Bracket

Gradient Bar

Swap RGB and Swap Alpha

Hue Saturation Brightness Contrast Blur Squeeze Cycle

Gradient Modifiers

The complete **Gradient Designer**.

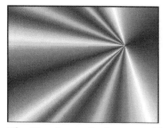

The **Preview window** provides a sample of what your gradient will look like, and allows you to reposition the origin of the gradient by dragging around the window.

The Gradient Designer elements

The **Gradient Bar** lets you pick colors for your gradients.

Pressing on the Gradient Bar displays the **Gradient Color Picker** which allows you to choose a Color, a Shade of Gray, or Opacity, or amount of transparency.

The **Gradient Modifiers** give you more control over Hue, Saturation, Brightness, Contrast, Blur, the center Squeeze, and rotation Cycle. Dragging from left to right on the dots affects these modifiers.

Gradient Designer

The Gradient Designer elements

The **Gradient Bracket** lets you define what area of the Gradient Bar you are working in. The Gradient Bracket can be resized by dragging on its ends.

Pressing on the **Swap RGB** and **Swap Alpha** triangles will display those choices.

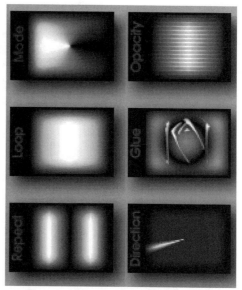

Pressing on the **Mode, Loop, Opacity,** or **Glue Control panels** displays the pop-up menus with the options for those panels.

Pressing on the **Opacity** or **Repeat Control panels**, and immediately dragging to the left or right, changes the setting of the panel. Dragging to the right increases the setting. Dragging to the left decreases the setting.

Pressing and dragging within the **Direction Control panel** allows you to change the direction of the effect.

The Texture Explorer elements

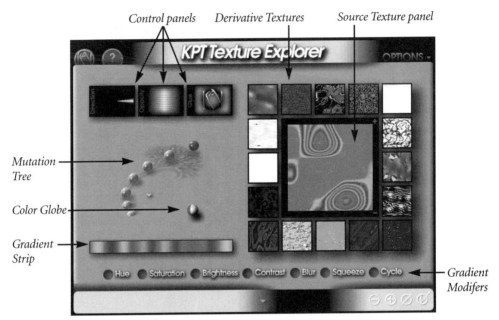

The complete **Texture Explorer**.

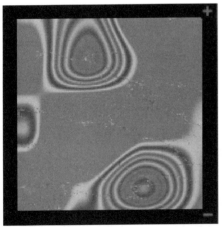

The **Source Texture panel** shows you the current texture. Pressing and dragging on the Source Texture panel lets you slide the texture within the panel.

The **Derivative Textures** are located around the edge of the Source Texture panel.

The Texture Explorer elements

The **Color Globe** controls the gradients used in the Derivative Textures. Clicking on the Color Globe randomizes each of the gradients.

The **Mutation Tree** controls the amount of mutation applied to the Derivative Textures. Moving the mouse toward the higher balls of the Mutation Tree increases the amount of mutation. Clicking applies the new mutations.

The **Gradient Strip** displays the gradient currently being used for the source texture. Pressing on the Gradient Strip displays the list of gradient presets available.

Hue Saturation Brightness Contrast Blur Squeeze Cycle

The **Gradient Modifiers** give you more control over Hue, Saturation, Brightness, Contrast, Blur, the center Squeeze, and roation Cycle. Dragging from left to right on the little dots affects these modifiers.

The Texture Explorer elements

Pressing and dragging within the **Direction Control panel** allows you to change the direction of the texture.

The **Opacity Control panel** lets you choose different sample images to test how your gradient will finally appear. Press on the Opacity Control panel and immediately drag to the left or right, to change the opacity of the gradient. Dragging to the right increases the opacity, making the the gradient less transparent. Dragging to the left will make the gradient more transparent.

The **Glue Control panel** allows you to select different options as to how the gradient will interact with the background image. Pressing on the panel displays a pop-up menu with the options. Pressing and immediately dragging to the right or left will also display each of the options in the Preview Window.

Texture Explorer

The Interform elements

Mother panel *Offspring panel* *Father panel*

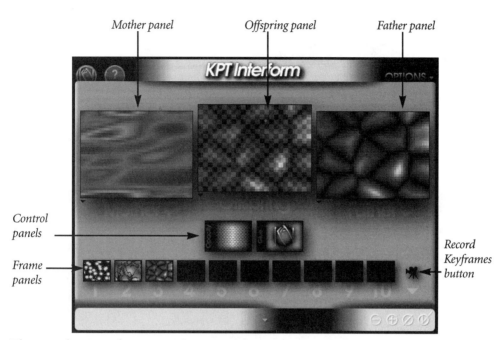

Control panels

Frame panels

Record Keyframes button

The complete **Interform** controls.

Interform

The Interform elements

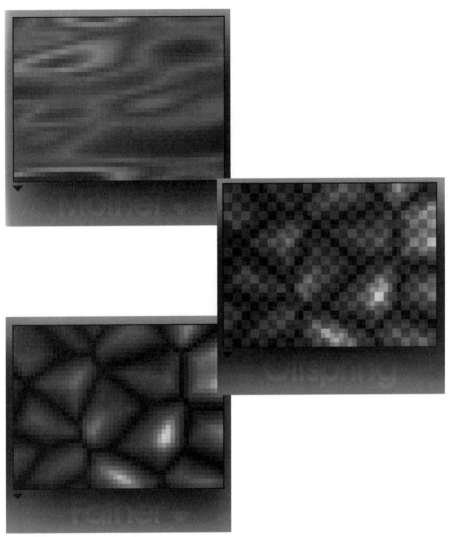

The **Mother** and **Father panels** display the current textures being applied to the Offspring panel. Pressing on the name of the Mother or Father panels, or the white triangle next to the name, displays the presets from the Texture Explorer.

Pressing on the black **Motion Triangles** displays the **UniMotion™ Options** that control the movement of each texture in the Interform process. Pressing and dragging on the Mother or Father panels will increase or decrease the speed of the motion.

The Interform elements

The **Opacity Control panel** lets you choose different sample images to test how your Interform effect will finally appear. Press on the Opacity Control panel and immediately drag to the left or right, to change the opacity of the effect. Dragging to the right will make the effect less transparent. Dragging to the left will make it more transparent.

The **Frame panels** are used to store frames of a Quick Time movie that is created from the interaction of the Mother and Father panels.

The **Glue Control panel** allows you to select different options as to how the gradient will interact with the background image. Pressing on the panel displays a pop-up menu with the options. Clicking on the panel cycles through each of the options. For an illustration of what each of the ten options looks like, see Chapter 12, "Apply Modes."

The **Record Keyframes button** brings up a Save dialog box which lets you save the animation as a Quick Time movie. The white triangle under the Record Keyframes button displays a pop-up menu with options for the movie.

The Compact Filters elements

While each of these filters create different effects, they all share a common interface.

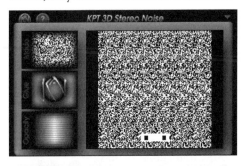
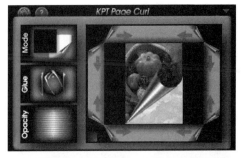
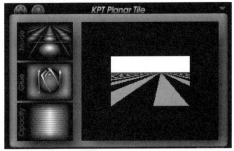
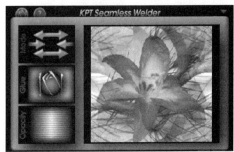

The **Compact Filters**: 3D Stereo Noise, Planar Tile, Twirl, Glass Lens, Page Curl, Seamless Welder, Video Feedback, and Vortex Tile.

Compact Filters

The Compact Filters elements

Clicking on the **Mode Control panel** will display each of the options. Pressing on the Mode Control panel displays the pop-up menu that allows you to choose from the different options for that particular filter.

Each of the Compact Filters has a **Preview window** where you can see a preview of the effect.

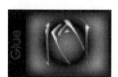

The **Glue Control panel** allows you to select different options as to how the gradient will interact with the background image. Pressing on the panel displays a pop-up menu with the options. Clicking on the panel will cycle through each of the options. For an illustration of what each of the options looks like, see Chapter 12, "Apply Modes."

Press on the **Opacity Control panel** and immediately drag to the left or right to change the opacity of the effect being created. Dragging to the right will make the effect less transparent. Dragging to the left will make it more transparent.

Compact Filters

The Lens f/x elements

These are six basic filters: Pixel f/x,
Gaussian f/x, Edge f/x, Intensity f/x,
Smudge f/x, Noise f/x plus the bonus filter
called MetaToys f/x. While each of these
filters create different effects, they all share
a common interface. This interface is
designed to resemble the controls on a
camera lens.

The **Preview button**
lets you toggle
between seeing the
center of the
selection and seeing
the area of the screen
that the lens is
currently over.

Pressing the
Options Gauge
gives you a pop-
up menu of the
options for the
current effect.
(This gauge is
not active for all
effects.)

The **Direction Control
Ball** allows you to
control in what direction
the effect is applied.

The **Intensity** and
**Opacity Control
Balls** let you
adjust how much
the effect will be
applied. Dragging
these around the
lens increases or
decreases the
effect.

Clicking the
Reset button
sets all the
controls back to
their default
setting.

Clicking on the
Glue Gauge
cycles you
through the
different Apply
modes. Pressing
on the gauge
shows a pop-up
menu of the
available modes.

Clicking on the **Mode Gauge**
cycles you through the different
modes for each of the filters.
Pressing on the gauge shows a
pop-up menu of the available
modes.

A sample of the **Lens f/x** interface.

Lens f/x

Common elements

While many of the filters look quite different, most share certain common controls. The size, shape, and position of each of these elements may change from filter to filter, but their basic functions remain the same.

The **Kai Logo**. In general, clicking on the logo will black out the interface and show you a full-screen preview or will simplify the preview in the interface.

The **Help button** is usually found next to the Kai Logo in each of the filters. Clicking on the Help button will launch the on-line help system.

Most of the filters have an **Options** pop-up menu located near the upper right-hand corner of the filter.

Clicking the **Cancel button** releases you from the filter and restores you to the host application. For some of the filters the Cancel button is a circle with a slash. For others it is a small red dot.

Clicking the **OK button** applies the current settings to your image. For some of the filters the OK button is a circle with a check mark. For others it is a green dot.

Clicking the **Add Preset button** (circle with plus sign) brings up a dialog box where you can give your current settings a name and store them. Clicking the **Delete Preset button** (circle with a minus sign) will activate the Presets Manager where you can delete presets as well as other preset features.

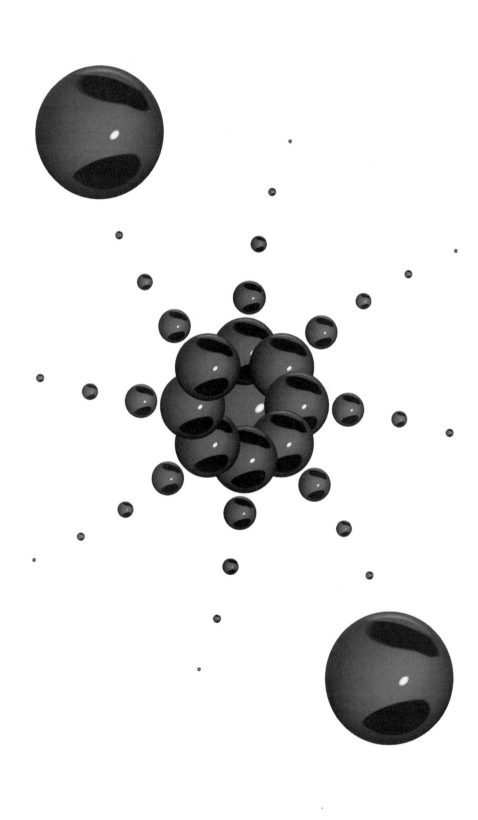

SPHEROID DESIGNER 4

You may think it's a simple thing, but the process of creating a sphere consists of many decisions. Is the sphere a beach ball or a ball bearing? What kind of light is shining on it? Bright? Colored? Spotlight or candle? Is there some sort of texture on the sphere? And finally, is it a single sphere or part of a group? And if the sphere is part of a group, is it randomly arranged or in a pattern? With all these possibilities you can understand why the Spheroid Designer of Kai's Power Tools is such a sophisticated filter.

In this chapter you will learn

◆ Preparing a file and launching the Spheroid Designer through the host application.

◆ Clearing previous settings in the Spheroid Designer.

◆ Making a plain sphere and adjusting its colors, lighting and surface.

◆ Saving your settings using the Memory Dots and the Presets.

◆ Using the Preset menu to choose settings.

◆ Adding and adjusting the bump maps to create textures in a sphere.

◆ Adjusting the curvature of a sphere.

◆ Adjusting the transparency of a sphere.

◆ Creating multiple spheres with the Apply Bubbles and Apply menu.

◆ Varying spheres using the Mutation Tree.

Spheroid Designer

The best way to master the Spheroid Designer is to start with a simple sphere. In this case you will create a red plastic ball. The ball will have a simple light shining on it.

Preparing to make a plain sphere

1. With the host application open, start a blank file (**Figure 1**).

2. Make the height and width of the file equal. Do not make a selection inside the blank file.

3. Choose KPT Spheroid Designer 3.0 from the KPT 3.0 menu (**Figure 2**).

4. You will now work inside the Spheroid Designer. You will not go back to the host application until you are done.

Tip

◆ If the height and width of the file are not equal, your sphere will be distorted.

◆ If you create a selection inside the blank file, the sphere will take on the dimensions of the selection.

◆ If your host application has layers, you can create your sphere on a layer.

◆ You must have some sort of image on a layer for Kai's Power Tools to work.

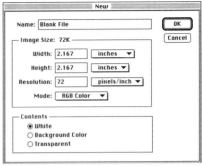

Figure 1. *Use the **host application** to create a blank file. Make the height and width equal so that your sphere is not distorted.*

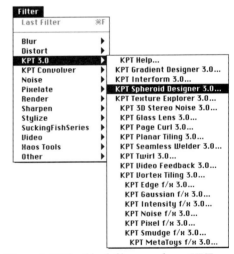

Figure 2. *With a blank file open, choose **KPT Spheroid Designer 3.0** from the **KPT 3.0** menu. This will be located in whatever menu you use to access Photoshop filters.*

Preparing to make a plain sphere

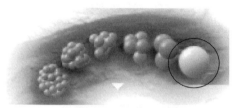

Figure 3. *To clear the Bump Map panel, open the* **Bump Map Presets** *by pressing on the* **small white triangle** *to the left of the panel. Choose* **None (Smooth Plastic)** *from the top of the list.*

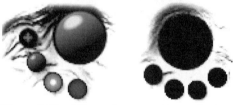

Figure 4. *Choose the* **single Apply Bubble** *to create only one sphere.*

Figure 5. *The difference between a* **Lamp** *that is* **turned on** *(left) and a* **Lamp** *that is* **turned off** *(right).*

The default settings of the Spheroid Designer depend on how the program was last used. If you are trying to create a plain sphere you will need to clear the Spheroid Designer of some of the settings.

Clearing the Spheroid Designer settings

1. To clear any bump map textures that may be active, press on the Bump Map menu next to the Bump Map panel. Choose **None (Smooth Plastic)** from the top of the preset list (**Figure 3**).

2. To create only one sphere make sure that the Make 1 Spheroid (single red ball) from the Apply Bubbles is active (**Figure 4**).

3. To create a single source of light, click on each of the lamps under the Preview Sphere so that only the left lamp is turned on (**Figure 5**).

4. Make sure the Light Polarity is a plus (+) sign so that the light reflects out from the sphere.

5. You should now have a plain sphere that can be lit and colored as desired.

6. Click the OK button to put the sphere into your blank file (**Figure 6**) or continue with the next steps.

Tips

◆ If you want to keep working in the Spheroid Designer, but want see a full-screen preview of the sphere you are creating, click on the Kai Logo in the upper left corner.

◆ When you are finished viewing your preview, click to leave the preview.

Figure 6. *The results of creating a* **plain sphere** *with only one lamp.*

Once you have a plain sphere, you will want to change its color. This is accomplished by changing the light that shines on the sphere.

Coloring a plain sphere

1. There are three places where you can change the color of your sphere.

2. Press on the small Global Dot in the lower left corner of the Designer for the Diffuse Hue RGB (**Figure 7**). Move the eyedropper over to a dark red color. The RGB values in the Info Area should read around 202, 9, 0.

3. Press on the Global Dot for the Ambient Hue RGB (**Figure 7**). Move the eyedropper over to a slightly darker red color. The RGB values in the Info Area should read around 106, 11, 0.

4. If the Preview Sphere is not red, you will need to change the color of the Lamp that is turned on.

5. Press on the Lamp Control Dot for Light Hue in RGB (**Figure 8**). Move the eyedropper around the rim of the Color Wheel to the white area (**Figure 9**). The Info Area should read around 220, 220, 220.

6. Click the OK button to put the sphere into your blank file or continue with the next steps.

Tip

◆ Hold the Option key as you press on any of the Control buttons that show the Color Wheel. This will give you the Apple Color Wheel rather than the MetaTools Color Wheel.

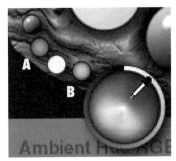

Figure 7. *Press on the **Diffuse Hue** (A) or **Ambient Hue** (B) Control buttons to access the Color Wheel.*

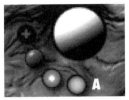

Figure 8. *Pressing on the **Light Hue in RGB** lamp control (A) lets you change the color of that lamp.*

Figure 9. *Dragging the eyedropper around the **rim** of the **Color Wheel** allows you to pick up black, white, or shades of gray.*

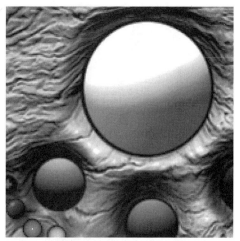

Figure 10. *Drag on the **Preview Sphere** or the **Lamp** to change the direction of the light that is shining on the sphere.*

Once you have colored your sphere, you may find that you would like to adjust the light that is shining on it.

Changing the direction of the light

1. Since your sphere has only one Lamp turned on, dragging on either the Lamp or the Preview Sphere will create the same effect.

2. Drag on the Preview Sphere to change the direction of the Lamp (**Figure 10**).

3. Click the OK button to put the sphere into your blank file or continue with the next steps.

Tip

◆ The sphere you are manipulating only has one side. So, unlike the real world, when you drag to the edge of the sphere the light immediately appears on the other side rather than traveling all around the back of the sphere.

Changing the lighting can also change your sphere to a more matte surface.

Creating a matte surface

1. Press on the Highlight Intensity Control button (**Figure 11**). To create a more matte-like surface, drag to the left to lower the amount to 0%.

3. If your sphere looks too dark at this point, press on the Light Intensity Control button (**Figure 11**), and drag to the right to increase the light.

4. If your sphere still looks too dark, you may want to adjust the direction of the light on the sphere.

5. Click the OK button to put the sphere into your blank file (**Figure 12**) or continue with the next steps.

You can also use the lighting controls to create a more shiny or polished surface.

Creating a shiny surface

1. Press on the Highlight Intensity Control button. To create a shinier surface, drag to the right to increase the amount to 50%.

2. Press on the Light Intensity Control button. Drag to set the Light Intensity to around 150%.

3. Press on the Ambient Intensity and the Light Diffusion Control buttons of the Small Global Dots to make further adjustments to the surface of the sphere.

4. Click the OK button to put the sphere into your blank file (**Figure 13**) or continue with the next steps.

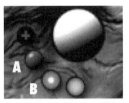

Figure 11. *The **Light Intensity** (**A**) and **Highlight Intensity** (**B**) controls let you change the surface of a sphere from matte to shiny.*

Figure 12. *Lowering the Highlight Intensity results in a more matte-like surface.*

Figure 13. *Increasing the Highlight Intensity and Light Intensity results in a shinier surface.*

Creating a matte surface; Creating a shiny surface

Figure 14. *Adding other lamps with other colors to the sphere results in a marble-like sphere.*

Once you have a plain sphere, you can add more light using the other three lamps. This allows you to create the effect of a sphere with different swirls of color.

Creating more colors in a sphere

1. Click on each of the black lamps to turn them on.

2. Set each of the lamps as follows:

Lamp #2:
Light Hue: Yellow 240, 225, 0.
Highlight Intensity: 85%.
Light Intensity: 200%

Lamp #3:
Light Hue: Blue 0, 38, 244.
Highlight Intensity: 100%
Light Intensity: 100%

Lamp #4:
Light Hue: Green 7, 112, 26.
Highlight Intensity: 65%.
Light Intensity: 180%

3. Drag on the Preview Sphere to change the direction of each of the four lamps. The lamps change their positions independently around the sphere, so the colors and highlights will move independently within the sphere. This will give the effect of your colors swirling in the sphere, similar to a marble (**Figure 14**).

4. To vary the look, change the Polarity of the yellow and green lamps from positive to negative. This creates darker areas within the colors.

5. Click the OK button to put the sphere into your blank file or continue with the next steps.

After you have created settings that you particularly like, you might want to use them again. There are two ways of saving your settings. One is the Memory Dots. The other is the Add Preset button.

Working with the Memory Dots

1. Once you have a sphere with settings that you want to save, click on one of the nine gray Memory Dots. The dot will turn from gray to gold, indicating that it is holding information (**Figure 15**).

2. If you have a gold Memory Dot, click on it to apply the stored settings. The dot will turn red indicating that it has been applied.

Tip

◆ To clear a Memory Dot, hold the Option key as you click on the dot. It will turn gray indicating that you can now store new settings in the dot.

Using the Add Preset button

1. Once you have a sphere with settings that you want to save, click on the Add Preset button (**Figure 16a**).

2. A dialog box will appear where you can enter the name of your setting (**Figure 16b**).

3. When you have named your preset, click OK. This will add your preset to the Preset menu.

Figure 15. *Clicking on a **Memory Dot** will turn it from gray to gold, saving the current settings.*

Figure 16a. *Click on the **Add Preset button** to save the current settings.*

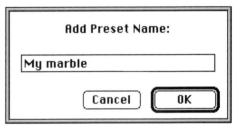

Figure 16b. *The **Add Preset Name** dialog box lets you give a name to your settings and store them with the presets.*

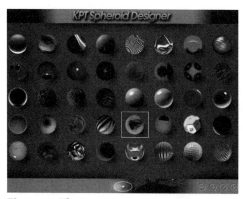

Figure 17. *The **Preset menu**. Moving your mouse over the sphere you want will select it with a rectangle. Clicking on a sphere with a rectangle will apply that preset to your sphere.*

There are 82 presets that come with the Spheroid Designer. These can be accessed through the Preset menu.

Using the Preset menu

1. Press on the small white triangle to the right of the Info Area. This will launch the graphical Preset menu.

2. The graphical Preset menu is a window that appears over the Spheroid Designer and displays representations of each of the stored presets.

3. If your mouse is moved outside the top or bottom of this screen, the Preset menu will scroll to display more presets.

4. To stop the scrolling, move your mouse inside the window.

5. When you find a preset that you like, move your mouse over it. A rectangle will appear around the sphere (**Figure 17**).

6. Click on a preset with a rectangle around it to apply it to your sphere. This will release you from the Preset menu.

Tips

◆ Click anywhere outside the preset area to return to the main window without applying a preset.

◆ If you prefer to pick your presets from a written list, you can change the Preferences or hold the spacebar as you click on the triangle to launch the Preset menu.

Not only can you create smooth surfaces for your spheres, but you can add surface patterns. These are called Bump Maps. The Spheroid Designer has 26 built-in bump maps.

Adding a bump map to a sphere

1. Start with a plain, single-colored sphere. This will allow you to see the results of adding the Bump Map more clearly.

2. Press on the Bump Map menu triangle to the left of the Bump Map panel. Choose one of the bump maps listed. For this example, we will use the Golfoid map, which has a surface similar to a golf ball.

3. You will see the bump map in the Bump Map panel and on the Preview Sphere (**Figure 18**).

Figure 18. *The **Bump Map panel** displays the current bump map.*

Figure 19. *The difference between setting a **Zoom Amount of 100%** (left) and setting a **Zoom Amount of 80%** (right).*

Figure 20. *The difference between setting a **Bump Rotation of 0°** (left) and setting a **Bump Rotation of 45°** (right).*

Figure 21. *The difference between setting a **Bump Height of 80%** (left) and setting a **Bump Height of 20%** (right).*

Figure 22. *The difference between setting a **positive Bump Polarity** (left) and setting a **negative Bump Polarity** (right).*

Choosing the bump map will change the appearance of your sphere. However, depending on how the program was last used, the sphere may or may not resemble a golf ball. To finish your work, you will need to make further adjustments to the bump map.

Adjusting the bump map

1. To change the size of the bump map, press on the Bump Zoom Control button. Drag to the left to decrease the zoom. Drag to the right to increase the zoom. If you are watching the Info Area, the Zoom Amount should be around 80% (**Figure 19**).

2. To change the orientation of the bump map, press on the Bump Rotation Control button. Drag to the left or right to change the angle listed in the Info Area (**Figure 20**).

3. To change how deep the bump map effect is applied to the sphere, press on the Bump Height Control button. Drag to the right to increase the depth. Drag to the left to decrease the depth. If you are watching the Info Area, the Bump Height Amount should be around 80% (**Figure 21**).

4. You can also change the way a bump map moves in or out of a sphere. Click on the Bump Polarity Control button to make sure the map is positive. This will give the appearance of the indentations in a golf ball (**Figure 22**).

5. Click the OK button to put the golf ball into your file or continue with the next steps.

Adjusting a bump map

In addition to the bump maps, the Sphere Curvature in the Global Controls will change the appearance of the sphere.

Adjusting the Sphere Curvature

1. Press on the Sphere Curvature Global Control.

2. Drag to the right to increase the curvature. As you increase the curvature you will see the bump map become more distorted (**Figure 23**).

3. Drag to the left to decrease the curvature. If you decrease the curvature below 0%, the effect will be as if you had cut open the sphere and flattened its surface out.

4. Click the OK button to put the sphere into your file (**Figure 24**) or continue with the next steps.

Figure 23. *The difference between setting a* **Curvature of 100%** *and its* **Curvature Control button** *(left) and setting a* **Curvature of 20%** *and its* **Curvature Control button** *(right).*

Figure 24. *The plain sphere transformed into a golf ball by adding a bump map.*

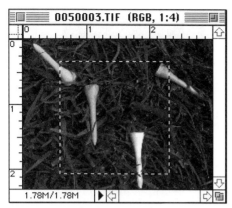

Figure 25. *Creating a* **square selection** *in a rectangular image ensures the sphere will be circular, not elliptical.*

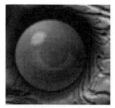

Figure 26. *As you increase the amount of the* **Transparency Global Control** *you will see an eye appear.*

Figure 27. *The results of increasing the transparency behind the sphere. In this case it created the look of a glass golf ball.*

So far your spheres have had no transparency. If you have a file with an image in it, then adjusting the transparency of the sphere will allow the image to be added to the sphere.

Adjusting the transparency of a sphere

1. Start with a file with an image in it.
2. If you would like the sphere to fill only a certain portion of the image, use a selection tool that will cover the area you want the sphere to cover. If your selection is not a square or circle, then the sphere you create will be an elliptical sphere (**Figure 25**).
3. Choose KPT Spheroid Designer 3.0 from the KPT 3.0 menu.
4. Follow the previously described steps to create whatever sphere you would like.
5. Once you are satisfied with the sphere, press on the Transparency sphere of the Global Controls. Drag to the right to increase the transparency, and thus let more of the image blend with the sphere. Drag to the left to decrease the transparency (**Figure 26**).
7. Click the OK button to put the sphere into your file (**Figure 27**) or continue with the next steps.

Tips

◆ When the transparency feature is used, the image will be applied onto the surface of the sphere and will be distorted according to the Sphere Curvature settings.

◆ A transparency setting of 100% will cause the image to be distorted without applying any of the features of the sphere.

◆ If you click on the Kai Logo to preview your sphere, you will not see the effects of any transparency setting.

Transparency

After you have made one sphere, you may want to create many spheres at once. This is where you can use the Apply Bubbles.

Creating multiple spheres in a random pattern

1. Once you have a sphere that you like, you can create multiples of that sphere using the Apply Bubbles.

2. To create 500 spheres, click on the Apply Bubble that is fifth from the right.

3. Press on the small white triangle under the Apply Bubbles to view the Apply menu. These are the options as to how your spheres will be arranged (**Figure 28**).

4. To create a random arrangement of size and position where your spheres will not overlap, choose Apollonian Packing. To create a random arrangment of size and position where your spheres will overlap, choose Random Spheres (**Figure 29**).

Tip

◆ Apply choices in the Spiral, Star, Splatter, and Radial Spherize modes will not show their patterns unless 500 or more spheres are chosen using the Apply Bubbles.

◆ If you choose the Use Shadows option, your spheres will cast shadows onto their background.

◆ If you choose the Use Mutation option, multiple spheres will appear with random mutations based on the settings in the Mutation Tree (see following page).

Apollonian Packing
Random Spheres
Random Ellipses
Spiral Packing1
✓ Spiral Packing2
Spiral Packing3
Star Packing1
Star Packing 2
Splatter Small
Splatter Medium
Splatter Big
Radial Spherize
Genesis Packing
Use Shadows
Use Mutation
Spheres on a Path
Genesis Editor...

Figure 28. *The **Apply menu** choices.*

Figure 29. *The results of choosing **50 spheres** arranged using the **Random Spheres** setting.*

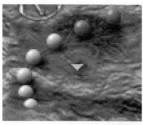

Figure 30. *The higher you click on the balls of the* ***Mutation Tree****, the more the sphere will change.*

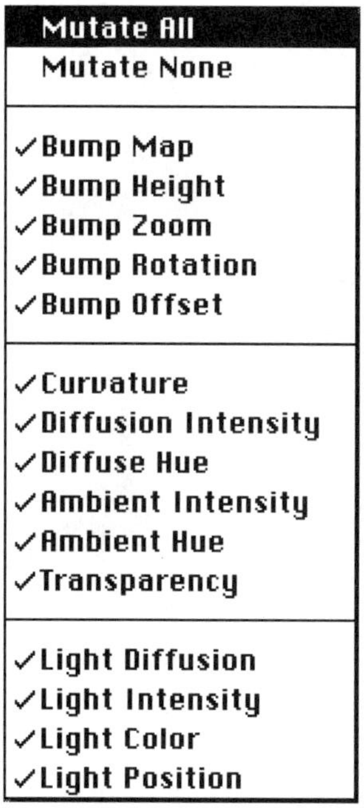

Mutate All
Mutate None
✓ **Bump Map**
✓ **Bump Height**
✓ **Bump Zoom**
✓ **Bump Rotation**
✓ **Bump Offset**
✓ **Curvature**
✓ **Diffusion Intensity**
✓ **Diffuse Hue**
✓ **Ambient Intensity**
✓ **Ambient Hue**
✓ **Transparency**
✓ **Light Diffusion**
✓ **Light Intensity**
✓ **Light Color**
✓ **Light Position**

Figure 31. *The options for the* ***Mutation Tree****.*

In addition to creating spheres by setting the controls the way you want, you can also create variations on your spheres using random mutations generated by the Mutation Tree.

Using the Mutation Tree

1. Drag your mouse over the balls of the Mutation Tree. The higher you drag up the tree, the more your sphere will be mutated (**Figure 30**). The balls will turn from brown to red indicating how much of a mutation you will create.

2. Click on the last red ball and notice how your sphere will have changed.

3. Press on the small white triange under the Mutation Tree. This will display the options for the mutations (**Figure 31**).

4. Select from the Mutation pop-up menu which attributes you want to mutate when you click on the balls of the Mutation Tree.

GRADIENT DESIGNER

The technical term gradient refers to any blend between two colors or tints of a color. With the KPT Gradient Designer, though, you can bend, twist, multiply, and otherwise manipulate blends into complete works of art. You can add KPT gradients to the background of an existing image or use them to create complete artworks. For example, the artwork on the facing page was created entirely within the Gradient Designer.

In this chapter you will learn

◆ Preparing a file and launching the Gradient Designer through the host application.

◆ Clearing previous settings in the Gradient Designer.

◆ Choosing the colors and direction of the gradient.

◆ Two methods for increasing the repetitions of the gradient.

◆ Using the Gradient Bracket.

◆ Selecting grays and transparencies.

◆ Using the Opacity Control panels.

◆ Creating bursts, shapebursts, pathbursts, radial sweeps, gradients on a path and grayscale mapbursts.

◆ Modifying a gradient using the Loop Control panel.

◆ Using the Gradient Modifiers.

◆ Working with the Presets menu.

◆ Working with the Swap RGB and Swap Alpha presets.

To begin working with the Gradient Designer, you should start with a simple three-color gradient.

Preparing to make a gradient

1. With the host application open, start a blank file (**Figure 1**).

2. Choose KPT Gradient Designer 3.0 from the KPT 3.0 menu (**Figure 2**).

3. You will now work inside the Gradient Designer. You will not go back to the host application until you are done.

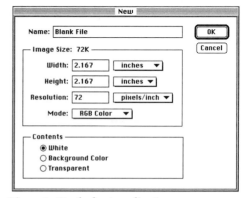

Figure 1. *Use the **host application** to create a blank file.*

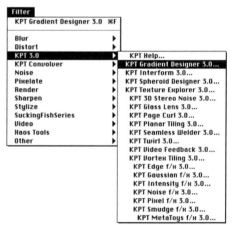

Figure 2. *With a blank file open, choose **KPT Gradient Designer 3.0** from the **KPT 3.0** menu. This will be located in whatever menu you use to access Photoshop filters.*

Preparing a file

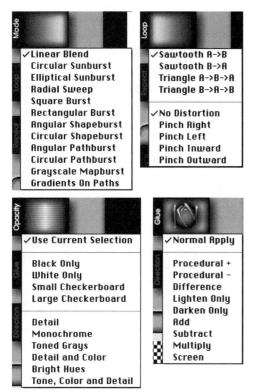

Figure 3. *Pressing anywhere on the **Mode, Loop, Opacity,** or **Glue Control panels** displays their submenus.*

The default settings of the Gradient Designer depend on how the program was last used. Before you create your simple gradient, you will need to clear some of the previous settings.

Clearing the Gradient Designer settings

1. Press on the Mode Control panel and choose Linear Blend from the pop-up menu (**Figure 3**).

2. Press on the Loop Control panel and choose Sawtooth A->B and No Distortion (**Figure 3**).

3. Press on the Opacity Control panel so that the pop-up menu reads Use Current Selection (**Figure 3**).

4. Press on the Glue Control panel so the pop-up menu reads Normal Apply (**Figure 3**).

5. Press on the Repeat Control panel so that the Info Area reads Repeat: 1 time(s) (**Figure 4**).

6. Press on the Direction Control panel and drag so that the Info Area angle reads 0° (**Figure 4**).

Figure 4. *Pressing on the **Repeat** or **Direction Control panels** displays their status in the **Info Area** at the bottom left of the **Gradient Designer**.*

Clearing the settings

At this point you only have whatever the default colors of your gradient were. You can now choose new colors for your gradient.

Choosing colors for a gradient

1. Move your mouse over to the left side of the Gradient Bar and press. This will display the Gradient Color Picker (**Figure 5**).

2. Still pressing down, move the eyedropper over to the Gradient Color Picker. Move the eyedropper to the middle so that the first color of the gradient is a light, sky blue. Let go of the mouse.

3. Move your mouse over to the right side of the Gradient Bar and press. Then move the eyedropper so that the last color of the gradient is a light yellow.

4. Move your mouse to the middle of the Gradient Bar and press. Then move the eyedropper so that the middle color of the gradient is a dark blue. You have just created a simple three-color, linear gradient (**Figure 6**).

Changing the direction and loop of the gradient

1. Drag on the Direction Control panel and move the indicator so that the Info Area reads around 50°. The indicator in the panel will show the angle you have chosen (**Figure 7**).

2. The new gradient will appear in the Preview window (**Figure 8**).

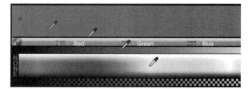

Figure 5. *Pressing on the **Gradient Bar** will display the **Gradient Color Picker**. Move the eyedropper to select a color.*

Figure 6. *A simple **Linear Gradient** will appear in the **Gradient Bar** and the **Preview window**.*

Figure 7. *Pressing and dragging on the **Direction Control panel** to change the angle of the gradient.*

Figure 8. *Changing the direction of a **Linear Gradient** shows the change in the **Preview window**.*

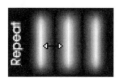

Figure 9. *Press on the **Repeat Control panel** and drag to the right to increase the number of repetitions.*

Figure 10. *After you have set the number of repetitions, if you click on the **Repeat Control panel** you will create those repetitions within the **Gradient Bar**.*

While your gradient has only three colors in it, you can still make those colors repeat. There are actually two ways to do this.

Increasing the repetitions (method #1)

1. Press on the Repeat Control panel and drag to the right (**Figure 9**).

2. As you drag, the number of repetitions will increase in the Repeat Control panel as well as in the Preview window.

3. If you want to lower the number of repetitions, drag to the left.

Increasing the repetitions (method #2)

1. Press on the Repeat Control panel and drag to the right to increase the number of repetitions.

2. When you have set the number of repetitions, click on the Repeat Control panel.

3. Each click will increase the number of repetitions of the colors within the Gradient Bar (**Figure 10**). The Repeat Control panel will reset to 1 repetition.

Tips

◆ The advantage of method #1 is that you can reverse the number of repetitions. The disadvantage is that you are limited to only 10 repetitions.

◆ The advantage of method #2 is that you can have hundreds of repetitions. The disadvantage is that you have to reset the Gradient Bar using the Color Picker to clear the repetitions.

To add more colors to the gradient, you will need to narrow the area along the Gradient Bar that you are working on. To do this you will use the Gradient Bracket.

Working with the Gradient Bracket

1. Using the simple gradient from the earlier exercises, press on the left "leg" of the Gradient Bracket.

2. Drag the leg to the right till it is over the dark blue, middle color of your gradient (**Figure 11**).

3. Press on the Gradient Bar within the bracketed area and choose a red color. Your gradient should now go from light blue to dark blue to red to yellow.

4. To add another color between the light blue and dark blue, you will need to move the Gradient Bracket.

5. Rather than move both the left and right legs of the bracket, you can drag the right leg all the way to the left side. This keeps the leg over the blue area at the same location.

6. With the Gradient Bracket over the light to dark blue area, press on the Gradient Bar and choose a green color.

7. Move the Gradient Bracket to different areas along the Gradient Bar to add other colors (**Figure 12**).

Tips

◆ To copy a color from one part of the gradient into the other, drag your eyedropper to that portion of the gradient.

◆ Work from the large areas and then to the smaller areas. This will keep you from erasing the colors you have already created.

◆ Double click on the flat top of the Gradient Bracket to reset it to stretch completely across the bar.

Figure 11. *Drag a leg of the **Gradient Bracket** to limit the area that you are working on.*

Figure 12. *Moving the **Gradient Bar** to different positions allows you to add multiple colors to the gradient.*

Figure 13. *The Grayscale Ramp above the colors lets you choose from black to white shades.*

Figure 14. *Pressing with the eyedropper on the checkerboard Opacity Ramp below the colors lets you create transparency effects.*

So far, all the colors you have chosen have been from the main area of the color bar. However, you can also pick shades of gray and transparencies using the Gradient Color Picker.

Selecting a shade of gray

1. With the Gradient Bracket positioned over a small area, press on the Gradient Bar and drag the eyedropper along the Grayscale Ramp just above the colors (**Figure 13**).

2. Moving the eyedropper to the left side creates darker grays. The left end of the ramp gives you black.

3. Moving the eyedropper to the right side creates lighter grays. The right end of the ramp gives you white.

You can also select transparent areas for your gradient. This will allow you to create holes in the gradient where the image in your original file will show through.

Selecting a transparency

1. With the Gradient Bracket positioned over a small area, press on the Gradient Bar and drag the eyedropper along the black and white checkerboard just below the colors. This is the Opacity Ramp (**Figure 14**).

2. Moving the eyedropper to the left side creates a less transparent area.

3. Moving the eyedropper to the right side creates a more transparent area.

4. You can also get a totally transparent area by moving the eyedropper over to the word None on the left side of the Gradient Color Picker.

In addition to making certain areas of your gradient opaque, you can adjust the opacity of the gradient as a whole.

Using the Opacity Control panel

1. Open a file that contains some sort of image.

2. Open the Gradient Designer and choose a gradient.

3. Press on the Opacity Control panel and choose Use Current Selection from the pop-up menu. You won't be able to see the image behind the gradient, though, until you lower the opacity.

4. Press on the Opacity Control panel and immediately drag to the right to lower the opacity (**Figure 15**). You see your image in the Preview window.

Tips

◆ If you get the pop-up menu, release and try again. You need to start your drag *very* quickly.

◆ For other ways to have your image interact with the gradient, see Chapter 12, "Apply Modes."

Figure 15. *Dragging the **Opacity Control panel** to the right lets you see the background image behind the gradient.*

Figure 16. *The difference between a three-color* **Circular Sunburst** *gradient (top), and an* **Elliptical Sunburst** *gradient (bottom).*

So far all the gradients you have made have been linear, that is they move along a line. However, there are several other modes that let you change the shape of your gradient.

Creating circular and elliptical sunbursts

1. Create a rectangular file or make a rectangular selection on your image so that it is wider than it is tall.

2. Open the Gradient Designer and make sure the Gradient Bar has at least three colors in it.

3. Press on the Mode Control panel and choose Circular Sunburst from the pop-up menu.

4. Click on the Kai Logo to see the full-screen preview. Click on the full-screen preview to go back to the Gradient Designer.

6. Press on the Mode Control panel and choose Elliptical Sunburst.

7. Click on the Kai Logo to see the full-screen preview (**Figure 16**).

Tip

◆ If your image or selected area is a square, you will see very little difference between the Circular and Elliptical Sunbursts.

Circular and elliptical sunbursts

Creating square and rectangular bursts

1. Create a rectangular file or make a rectangular selection on your image so that it is wider than it is tall.

2. Open the Gradient Designer and make sure the Gradient Bar has at least three colors in it.

3. Press on the Mode Control panel and choose Square Burst from the pop-up menu.

4. Click on the Kai Logo to see the full-screen preview.

5. Press on the Mode Control panel and choose Rectangular Burst.

6. Click on the Kai Logo to see the full-screen preview.(**Figure 17**).

Tip

◆ If your image or selected area is a square, you will see very little difference between the Square and Rectangular Bursts.

Figure 17. *The difference between a three-color* ***Square Burst*** *gradient (top), and a* ***Rectangular Burst*** *gradient (bottom).*

Another exciting gradient shape is the Radial Sweep. This is similar to the gradient that would be created by a radar scope.

Creating a radial sweep

1. Make sure the Gradient Bar has at least three colors.

2. Press on the Mode Control panel and choose Radial Sweep from the pop-up menu.

3. To see the effect of adding more colors, narrow the size of the Gradient Bracket and choose more colors from the Gradient Color Picker (**Figure 18**).

Figure 18. *A three-color* ***Radial Sweep*** *gradient.*

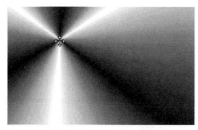

Figure 19. *Dragging with the **four-headed arrow** allows you to move the center of your gradient.*

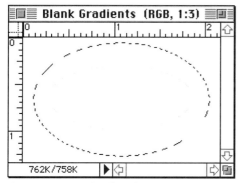

Figure 20. *To see the **Shapebursts**, create a selection on your blank file.*

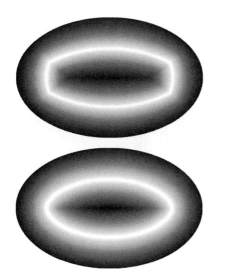

Figure 21. *The difference between an **Angular Shapeburst** gradient (top), and a **Circular Shapeburst** gradient (bottom).*

Some of the gradient modes allow you to change the center point of the gradient.

Changing the center of the gradient

1. Choose any of the Circular Sunburst, Elliptical Sunburst, Square Burst, Rectangular Burst, or Radial Sweep modes.

2. Move your mouse over the Preview window. You will see the cursor change to a four-headed arrow.

3. Press and drag on the Preview window and you will see the center of your gradient move (**Figure 19**).

The Gradient Designer also has modes for bursts that conform to the shape of your selection.

Creating angular and circular shapebursts

1. Because the effects of these modes are not obvious on rectangular selections, create an elliptical selection on your image (**Figure 20**).

2. Press on the Mode Control panel and choose Angular Shapeburst from the pop-up menu.

3. Click on the Kai Logo to see the full-screen preview. Notice how the transitions of the gradient can look somewhat abrupt.

5. Press on the Mode Control panel and choose Circular Shapeburst from the pop-up menu.

6. Click on the Kai Logo to see the full-screen preview. Notice how the transitions are smoother (**Figure 21**).

The Pathburst modes use your selection as a reference shape, but fill the entire image.

Creating angular and circular pathbursts

1. Create an elliptical selection on your image.

2. Press on the Mode Control panel and choose Angular Pathburst from the pop-up menu.

3. Click on the Kai Logo to see the full-screen preview. Notice how the image is filled, but the shape follows the selection.

5. Press on the Mode Control panel and choose Circular Pathburst from the pop-up menu.

6. Click on the Kai Logo to see the full-screen preview. Notice how the transitions are smoother.(**Figure 22**).

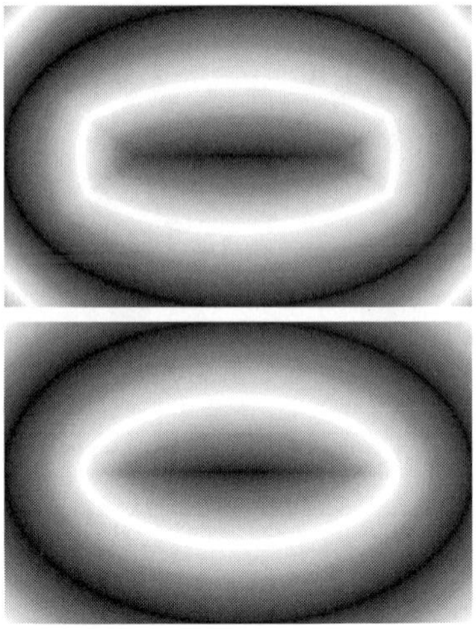

Figure 22. *The difference between a three-color **Angular Pathburst** gradient (top), and a **Circular Pathburst** gradient (bottom).*

You can also create neon effects using the Gradients on Paths.

Using the Gradients on Paths

1. In the host application, create a selected area on your image.

2. Apply a Feather Radius to your selection. The wider the feather the thicker your neon will be.

3. Create a three-color gradient that goes from dark to light to dark.

4. Press on the Mode Control panel and choose Gradients on Paths from the pop-up menu.

5. Click on the Kai Logo to see the full-screen preview. Notice how the gradient conforms to the shape of the path, but leaves a hole in the middle (**Figure 23**).

Figure 23. *In order to create the neon effect, apply the **Gradients on Paths** to a feathered selection.*

Angular and circular pathbursts; Gradients on Paths

Figure 24. *The right side of the image had the* ***Grayscale Mapburst*** *applied. This has applied the gradient in a certain manner depending on the colors of the original image.*

There is one more mode choice—the Grayscale Mapburst. To properly understand this mode, you will need to have some sort of image in your file. The gradient will be applied to your image according to the light and dark areas in the image. This is similar to making extreme changes to the color controls in a program such as Adobe Photoshop.

Creating a Grayscale Mapburst

1. Choose an image that has a wide range of dark and light areas.

2. Press on the Mode Control panel and choose Grayscale Mapburst from the pop-up menu.

3. If you do not see your image in the Preview window, press on the Opacity Control panel and choose Use Current Selection.

4. Make the left side of the gradient a dark color. Make the right side of the gradient a lighter color.

5. Set the repetitions for two or three.

6. Click on the Kai Logo to see a full-screen preview of the gradient. When you are satisfied with the effect, click the OK button (**Figure 24**).

Tip

◆ Although the mode is called Grayscale Mapburst, it works very well on colored images.

You can also change your gradient by adjusting the Loop Control panel. This controls both the order of the gradient and the rate of blending.

Adjusting the Loop controls

1. To best understand the effects of the Loop Control panel, start with a three or four-color linear gradient. Make sure the left and right sides are not the same colors.

2. Press on the Loop Control panel and examine the results of switching to from the Sawtooth A->B to the Sawtooth B->A to the Triangle A->B->A to the Triangle B->A->B setting (**Figure 25**).

3. With your gradient back on the original Sawtooth A->B setting, examine the results of changing the distortion settings from No Distortion to Pinch Right to Pinch Left to Pinch Inward to Pinch Outward (**Figure 26**).

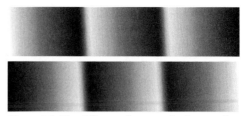

Figure 25. *The difference between the **Sawtooth A->B** mode (top) and the **Sawtooth B->A** mode (bottom).*

Figure 26. *The difference (from top to bottom) between the **No Distortion, Pinch Right, Pinch Left, Pinch Inward,** and **Pinch Outward** modes from the **Loop Control panel**.*

Loop controls

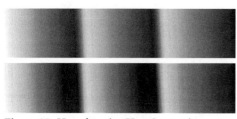

Figure 27. *How changing **Hue, Saturation, Brightness,** and **Contrast** modifiers affect a gradient.*

Figure 28. *How changing the **Blur** modifier affects a gradient.*

Figure 29. *How changing the **Squeeze** modifier affects a gradient.*

In addition to picking the colors for the gradients from the Gradient Color Picker, you can change the look of your gradient using the seven Gradient Modifiers.

Adjusting the Gradient Modifiers

1. Make sure the Gradient Bracket is over just the area that you want to change.

2. Press on the Hue, Saturation, Brightness, or Contrast modifiers and drag left or right to change those attributes of the colors (**Figure 27**).

3. Press on the Blur modifier and drag to the right. This will blur or feather the transition between your colors (**Figure 28**).

4. Press on the Squeeze modifier and drag to the left or right to squeeze the gradient to one side or the other. Using the Squeeze modifier always starts the squeeze at the center of the bracket (**Figure 29**). (See Tip immediately following for how to make an off-center squeeze.)

5. Press on the Cycle modifier and drag to the left or right to reposition the gradient within the Gradient Bar. If your left and right colors were not the same, you will see a sharp dividing line when you reposition the gradient.

Tip

◆ To squeeze a gradient from a point other than the center, hold the Option key and press down on that point. Then drag to the left or right.

Once you have a gradient that you like, you will want to save its settings.

Using the Add Preset button

1. Click on the Add Preset button.
2. A dialog box will appear where you can enter the name of your setting and choose a category (or name your own) where you want to store your gradient (**Figure 30**).
3. When you have named your preset, click OK. This will add your preset to the Preset menu.

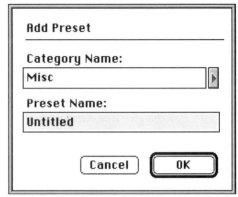

Figure 30. *The **Add Preset** dialog box lets you give a name to your settings and choose a category to store them in.*

The Gradient Designer ships with over 350 built-in presets. These can be accessed through the Preset menu.

Using the Preset menu

1. Press on the small white triangle to the right of the Info Area.
2. The graphical Preset menu displays representations of each of the stored presets.
3. Move your mouse outside the top or bottom of the Preset menu to display all the presets.
4. To stop the scrolling, move your mouse inside the window.
5. When you find a preset that you like, move your mouse over it. The gradient will light up (**Figure 31**).
6. Click on a lighted preset to apply it to your gradient.

Tips

◆ Click anywhere outside the preset area to return to the main window without applying a preset.

◆ To pick your presets from a written list, change the Preferences setting or hold the spacebar as you press on the triangle to launch the Preset menu.

Figure 31. *The **Preset menu** is opened by pressing on the white triangle. Moving your mouse over the gradient you want will select it. Clicking on a selected gradient will apply that preset to your gradient.*

Figure 32. *Applying the Swap RGB changes the colors of a gradient (top and bottom) without affecting any other attributes.*

Figure 33. *Applying the Swap Alpha changes the opacity of a gradient (top and bottom) without affecting any other attributes.*

When you choose a preset, you are choosing both the colors and opacity settings. If you want, you can choose just the colors in the presets or the opacity. This is done through the Swap RGB and Swap Alpha triangles.

Using the Swap RGB presets

1. Hold the spacebar and press on the Preset menu at the bottom of the Gradient Designer. Choose a Full Intensity Hue Spectrum from the Texture Blends submenu.

2. Move the center of the radial sweep to the upper left quadrant of the preview window. And change the Repeat Control panel to Repeat: 3 time(s).

3. You now need to change the colors in the gradient to those in another preset. But you do not want to lose the current position and repetitions.

4. Hold the spacebar as you press on the Swap RGB triangle on the right side of the Gradient Bar.

5. Choose Santa Fe from the Basic Gradients submenu. You have changed the colors, but not any other settings (**Figure 32**).

Using the Swap Alpha presets

1. The Swap Alpha triangle allows you to change the alpha channels or opacity settings in the Gradient Bar without affecting the colors in the Gradient Bar (**Figure 33**).

Tip

◆ If you do not hold the spacebar, you will see thumbnails of the Swap RGB and Swap Alpha presets in the Preset Manager. You can then pick a preset by moving your mouse over the preset you want.

River in cyberspace ©1996 S. Cohen

TEXTURE EXPLORER 6

Spheres and gradients you design, but textures, you *explore!* The Texture Explorer generates infinite varieties of textures and backgrounds. The real skill in working with the Texture Explorer is not how many different textures you can make. It means being able to control the features of your textures.

But that's not all. While most people think of textures as backgrounds, you can also use the Texture Explorer to create designs. For instance, the artwork on the facing page used the Texture Explorer to create both the background and foreground elements.

In this chapter you will learn

◆ Changing the Source Texture.

◆ Controlling the mutations.

◆ Changing colors with the Color Globe.

◆ Using the Gradient Bar.

◆ Moving the Source Texture.

◆ Changing the texture size and direction.

◆ Changing the opacity.

◆ Protecting a Derivative Texture.

◆ Working with Presets.

◆ Adjusting the Gradient Modifiers.

Preparing to make a texture

1. With the host application open, start with a blank file.

2. Choose KPT Texture Explorer 3.0 from the KPT 3.0 menu.

3. You will now work inside the Texture Explorer. You will not go back to the host application until you are done.

Start by letting the Texture Explorer create a few random textures.

Changing the Source Texture

1. Once you have launched the Texture Explorer, you already have a Source Texture available in the Preview window.

2. Click on one of the 16 Derivative Texture windows located around the Preview window. The Derivative Texture you chose will take the place of the original Source Texture. And new Derivative Textures will be created (**Figure 1**).

Figure 1. *The Source Texture is located in the large Preview window which is surrounded by 16 smaller windows containing the Derivative Textures.*

The Derivative Textures are mutations of the Source Texture.

Controlling the mutations

1. Move your mouse across the Mutation Tree. As you pass over each of the balls they will change color from red to cyan or back to red. The more red balls the greater the mutations of the Derivative Textures will be (**Figure 2**).

2. Move your mouse over the lowest red ball. The Info Area should read Minimum Mutation.

3. Click on the red ball. You will see that the Derivative Textures are much closer to the Source Texture.

Figure 2. *Variations of the Mutation Tree from the lowest mutation amount (left) to the highest amount (right).*

Tip

◆ Click on the lowest red ball to mutate your texture. Each of the Derivative Textures will then be the closest to the Source Texture.

Mutate All
Mutate None
✓ Panning
✓ Rotation
✓ Scale
✓ Zoom
✓ Color
✓ Blending
✓ Opacity
✓ Texture

Figure 3. *Press on the small white triangle under the **Mutation Tree** to see the **Mutation Options** pop-up menu.*

Figure 4. *Click on the **Color Globe** to change just the colors of your texture.*

In addition to how great the mutations are, you can also control which features of the texture are being mutated.

Setting the Mutation Options

1. Press on the white triangle under the Mutation Tree. You will see a pop-up menu with the options for your mutations (**Figure 3**).

2. Choose which attributes of the texture you want to have affected by the Mutation Tree.

Tip

◆ Use the Mutation Options to fine tune a texture by turning off each of the options one at a time.

The Color Globe gives you a quick way to mutate only the colors in your texture.

Using the Color Globe

1. Fill the Preview window with the Source Texture that you like.

2. Instead of clicking on the Mutation Tree, click on the Color Globe to the right of the Mutation Tree (**Figure 4**).

3. Each time you click only the colors of the Derivative Textures will change. The basic shape, size, angle, etc. of the texture will remain the same.

4. Continue to click on the Color Globe to change the colors of the Derivative Textures.

5. When you find a color scheme that you like, click on that Derivative Texture. That will become the Source Texture.

Tip

◆ The colors of your textures are actually gradients from the Gradient Designer that are being distorted.

Mutation Options; Color Globe

Instead of relying on the mutations of the Color Globe to find the gradient you like, you can also access the stored gradients through the Gradient Bar.

Using the Gradient Bar

1. Press on the Gradient Bar. You will see a pop-up menu containing a list of all the presets from the Gradient Designer (**Figure 5**).

2. Choose the gradient you would like to apply to your texture.

3. This will apply the colors of that gradient to your pattern without changing any of the other attributes.

You can also move the Source Texture to see more of the texture.

Moving the Source Texture

1. Position your mouse inside the Preview window.

2. Press and drag to move the Source Texture (**Figure 6**).

3. Once you have found a position that you like for the texture, click on the Mutation Tree to create derivatives of this Source Texture.

Figure 5. *Press on the **Gradient Bar** below the Color Globe to see a pop-up menu of all the available **Gradient Presets**.*

Figure 6. *Press and drag with the **four-headed arrow** to reposition your texture within the **Preview window**.*

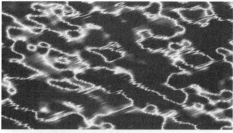

Figure 7. *The difference between a texture **before** scaling (top) and **after scaling** (bottom).*

Another way to change the look of your texture is to increase or decrease its size.

Changing the texture size

1. Click on the plus (+) sign in the upper right corner of the Preview window. The effect will be that you are zooming in on the image.

2. With each click you are creating a new texture pattern by scaling up the original texture (**Figure 7**).

3. Click on the minus (-) sign in the lower right corner of the Preview window. With each click you are creating a new texture pattern by scaling down the original texture.

4. Once the texture is sized to your satisfaction, click on the Mutation Tree to create derivatives based on this new size of the Source Texture.

Figure 8. *The difference between a texture **before** changing its direction (top) and **after changing the direction** (bottom).*

You can also vary your texture by changing its direction.

Changing the texture direction

1. Press on the Direction Control panel to rotate the Source Texture within the Preview window.

2. Once you have the direction of the texture that you like, click on the Mutation Tree to create derivatives based on this new direction of the Source Texture (**Figure 8**).

3. Each time you access a Derivative Texture, or apply one to the Source Texture, the Direction Control panel will reset to 0°.

Texture size; Texture direction

You can also adjust the opacity of your texture to let any image in your original file show through.

Using the Opacity Control panel

1. Open a file that contains some sort of image.

2. Open the Texture Explorer and choose a texture.

3. Press on the Opacity Control panel and choose Use Current Selection from the pop-up menu. You won't be able to see the image behind the texture, though, until you lower the opacity.

4. Press on the Opacity Control panel and immediately drag to the right to lower the opacity. You see your image in the Opacity Control panel as well as the Preview window (**Figure 9**).

5. When you apply the texture, you will see both the original image and the texture (**Figure 10**).

Tip

◆ If you get the pop-up menu when you press on the Opacity Control panel, release and try again. You must start your drag *very* quickly.

◆ For other ways to have your image interact with the texture, see Chapter 12, "Apply Modes."

Figure 9. *Press and drag very quickly to the left or right on the **Opacity Control panel** to change the how much of the original image is seen through the texture.*

Figure 10. *A plain image (top) and the same image after applying a **low opacity texture** (bottom).*

Figure 11. *The effect of changing* **Hue,** **Saturation, Brightness,** *and* **Contrast** *modifiers,* **before** *(top) and* **after** *(bottom).*

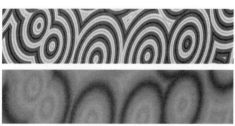

Figure 12. *The difference between a texture* **before** *applying the* **Blur** *(top) and* **after applying the** **Blur** *(bottom).*

Figure 13. *The difference between a texture* **before** *applying the* **Squeeze** *(top) and* **after applying** **the Squeeze** *(bottom).*

At the bottom of the Texture Explorer are a set of controls that are the same as the Gradient Modifiers in the Gradient Designer. These modifiers work similarly to their counterparts in the Gradient Designer.

Adjusting the Gradient Modifiers

1. Press on the Hue, Saturation, Brightness, or Contrast modifiers and drag left or right to change those attributes of the texture (**Figure 11**).

2. Press on the Blur modifier and drag to the right. This will blur or feather the pattern in your texture. (**Figure 12**).

3. Press on the Squeeze modifier and drag to the left or right to squeeze the texture pattern one way or the other (**Figure 13**).

4. Press on the Cycle modifier and drag to the left or right to reposition the gradient within the texture.

Gradient Modifiers

Once you have a Derivative Texture that you like, you can protect that texture from mutations.

Setting Texture Protection

1. When you see a Derivative Texture that you like, hold the Option key and click on the window for that Derivative Texture.

2. A red line will appear around the texture window (**Figure 14**). This indicates that the texture is protected. Any mutations or changes you make will not affect that texture.

3. To remove the protection from a Derivative Texture, hold the Option key as you click on the window. The texture will now change along with the rest of the Derivative Textures.

While protecting a Derivative Texture is useful for the current session, you need to use presets to save textures permanently.

Using the Add Preset button

1. Once you have a texture with settings that you want to save, click on the Add Preset button.

2. A dialog box will appear where you can enter the name of your setting (**Figure 15**).

3. When you have named your preset, click OK. This will add your preset to the Preset menu.

Figure 14. *Holding the Option key as you click on a **Derivative Texture** will set **Texture Protection** to that texture.*

Figure 15. *The **Add Preset Name** dialog box lets you give a name to your settings and store them with the presets.*

Figure 16. *The **Preset menu** is opened by pressing on the white triangle. Moving your mouse over the texture you want will select it. Clicking on a selected gradient will apply that preset to your gradient.*

Using the Preset menu

1. Pressing on the small white triangle to the right of the Info Area will launch the graphical Preset menu.

2. The graphical Preset menu is a window that appears over the Texture Explorer and displays representations of each of the stored presets.

3. If your mouse is moved outside the top or bottom of this screen, the Preset menu will scroll to display all the presets.

4. To stop the scrolling, move your mouse inside the window.

5. When you find a preset that you like, move your mouse over it. The box will have a white line around the texture (**Figure 16**).

6. Click on a highlighted preset to apply it to your gradient. This will release you from the Preset menu.

Tips

◆ Click anywhere outside the preset area to return to the main window without applying a preset.

◆ If you prefer to pick your presets from a written list, you can change the Preferences setting or you can hold the spacebar as you click on the triangle to launch the Preset menu.

Preset menu

INTERFORM 7

Most of the features of Kai's Power Tools are for creating static, or graphic images. However, Interform is different. Not only can you use it to create textured images for use in publishing and design, you can also use it to create QuickTime movies for use in all sorts of multi-media and applications. This chapter is divided into two parts.

The first part covers creating static images. You will learn

◆ Preparing a file and launching the Interform filter through the host application.

◆ Turning off the motion options.

◆ Creating an Offspring texture.

◆ Controlling the mixture between the Parent textures.

◆ Storing settings using Frames and Presets.

◆ Changing the opacity of the Offspring texture.

The second part covers animated images. You will learn

◆ Blending the textures using Manual and UniMotion Blending controls.

◆ Storing animated settings into frames.

◆ Setting the options for QuickTime movies.

◆ Recording QuickTime movies.

Interform

STATIC IMAGES

Preparing to create an Interform texture

1. With the host application open, start with a blank RGB file. (The file must be in the RGB mode or the Interform filter will not be available.)

2. Choose KPT Interform 3.0 from the KPT 3.0 menu (**Figure 1**).

3. You will now work inside the Interform filter. You will not go back to the host application until you are done.

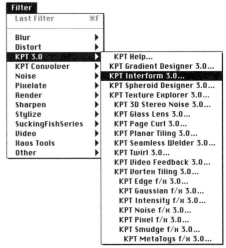

*Figure 1. With a blank file open, choose **KPT Interform 3.0** from the **KPT 3.0** menu. This will be located in whatever menu you use to access Photoshop filters.*

Most likely when you launch the Interform filter, you will see previews that are in motion. In order to understand how the Interform filter works, you should turn off the movement.

Turning off the motion options

1. Press on the small black triangle under the Mother panel and choose Manual Scooting. If the image in the Mother panel does not stop moving, click with your mouse right on the window.

2. Do the same for the Father panel.

3. If the image in the Offspring panel is still changing, press on the black triangle under that window and choose Manual Blending.

4. All three panels should now have static images (**Figure 2**).

*Figure 2. The **Mother, Father,** and **Offspring** panels of the Interform filter can have static or animated images.*

```
        ◆
Bees?
black pearl pond
black vinyl curtains
Bosch 1999
bubbles in space
bullets in giraffes
but is it OP art?
Castanets
CaveDwelling
CavePainting
Chagall's Driveway
ChannelFunnel
Christmas Molecules
Coins in the fountain
        ◆
```

Figure 3. *Press on the small white triangle next to the word Mother to display the pop-up menu of **Texture Explorer presets.***

Figure 4. *The **Offspring Preview panel** shows the combination texture created from the **Mother** and **Father** textures.*

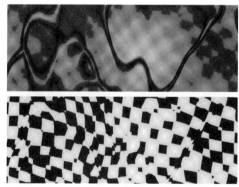

Figure 5. *The influence of the Mother and Father textures is varied by **changing the Interform amount**. In the top example the Father texture is more obvious. In the bottom example the Mother texture is more obvious.*

The Interform filter is a special way to take two textures from the Texture Explorer and combine them into a third. The original textures are called Mother and Father (Parent textures). The third texture is called the Offspring.

Creating an Offspring texture

1. Press on the white triangle next to the word Mother and choose one of the presets from the Texture Explorer (**Figure 3**). In this case we will use the "but is it OP art" preset.

2. Press on the triangle next to the word Father and choose the Dryadic Signature preset. Notice that the Offspring texture combines some of the attributes from both of the Parent textures (**Figure 4**).

To better understand the effect of using the Mother and Father textures to create the Offspring, you can change the amount of influence each parent has.

Changing the Influence of the Parent textures

1. Press on the Offsprint panel and drag to the right or left.

2. As you drag, the Info Area will show the Interform amount which can range from 0 to 100.

3. When the Interform amount is at 50 the influence of both of the Parent textures will be equal.

4. Dragging to the left lowers the Interform amount and increases the influence of the Father texture.

5. Dragging to the right increases the Interform amount and increases the influence of the Mother texture (**Figure 5**).

After you have created an Offspring texture that you particularly like, you might want to call it up again. There are two ways of saving your settings. One is the Frame panels. The other is the Add Preset button.

Working with the Frame panels

1. Once you have an Offspring with settings that you want to save, click on one of the ten black Frame panels at the bottom of the Interform window. The filled frame will show a preview of the texture (**Figure 6**).

2. If you have a filled frame, click on it to apply the stored settings.

Tip

◆ To clear a frame panel, hold the Option key as you click on the panel. It will turn black indicating that you can now store new settings in the frame.

Using the Add Preset button

1. Once you have an Offspring with settings that you want to save, click on the Add Preset button.

2. A dialog box will appear where you can enter the name of your setting (**Figure 7**).

3. When you have named your preset, click OK. This will add your preset to the Preset menu.

Figure 6. *Click on a blank **Frame panel** to store the current texture. Click on a filled panel to apply the stored setting.*

Figure 7. *The **Add Preset Name** dialog box lets you give a name to your settings and store them with the presets.*

Floaters
Golden Lovely
KaleidoWallpaper
Mosaic Flow
Purple AshFall
Rain Surreal
Reception?
RedRovers
Rosette-o-rama
Spikey
Trees'nEmbers
Water Ripples

Figure 8. *The **Preset pop-up menu** is opened by pressing on the white triangle in the middle of the Info Area.*

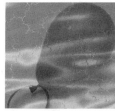

Figure 9. *A plain image (left) and the same image after applying a **low opacity Interform texture** (right).*

Interform ships with 12 built-in presets. These can be accessed through the Preset menu.

Using the Preset menu

1. Press on the small white triangle to the right of the Info Area. This will display the Preset pop-up menu.

2. Choose from the presets for the Offspring texture you want (**Figure 8**).

If you start with a file with some sort of image in it, adjusting the opacity of the Interform will allow the image already in the file to be added to the Offspring texture.

Using the Opacity Control panel

1. Open a file that contains some sort of image.

2. Open the Interform filter and choose a Mother and Father texture.

3. Press on the Opacity Control panel and choose Use Current Selection from the pop-up menu. You won't be able to see the image behind the texture, though, until you lower the opacity.

4. Press on the Opacity Control panel and immediately drag to the left to lower the opacity. (If you get the pop-up menu, release and try again. You need to start your drag *very* quickly.) Not only will you see your image in the preview window, you will see it in the Opacity Control panel (**Figure 9**).

Tip

◆ For other ways to have your image interact with the texture, see Chapter 12, "Apply Modes."

ANIMATED IMAGES

Once you've got a set of textures, you can then set them in motion. This will cause the Offspring texture to be formed using not just the images from the Parent textures but also their motions. There are several ways of adding motion to a Parent texture. The first is called Manual Scooting.

Adding Manual Scooting

1. Start with the static Offspring texture you created in the first part of this chapter. Press on the small black triangle under the either of the Parent textures. This displays the UniMotion Options (**Figure 10**). You will see that the Manual Scooting option is already on. However, the image is not moving.

2. Position your mouse inside the window of the Parent textures, and drag to the right. When you let go of the mouse, the Parent texture will start to move in the direction that you dragged.

3. Notice that the Offspring texture now shows the effect of the motion you just created.

4. Drag on the other Parent texture in a different direction. Notice that the Offspring texture now shows the effect of both motions (**Figure 11**).

✓Manual Scooting
Earthquake
Vibrate
Orbit
OrbitTheta
OrbitThetaSlow
OscillateVertical
OscillateHorizontal
Oscillate
Spiral
HorizontalSine
VerticalSine
HorizontalSineVary
VerticalSineVary
HorizontalSineVibe
VerticalSineVibe
Skating
HorizontalRubber
VerticalRubber
DiagonalRubber
HorizontalPullMe
VerticalPullMe
DiagonalPullMe

Figure 10. *The UniMotions pop-up menu.*

Figure 11. *The motions of both the Mother and Father textures are combined in the motion of the **Offsprint panel**.*

Animated Images
Manual Scooting

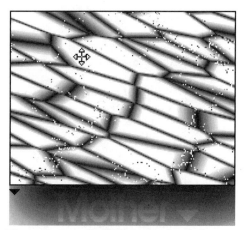

Figure 12. *Dragging with the **four-headed arrow** inside one of the Parent textures will set the intensity of the **UniMotion options.***

Manual Scooting only allows you motion in one direction. You can also use one of the 22 preset options that give you much more sophisticated animation effects.

Using the UniMotion Options

1. Press on the UniMotion pop-up menu for either Parent texture and choose one of the options listed under Manual Scooting.

2. Your Parent texture will begin to move in a preset pattern.

3. You will also see this change in the Offsprint panel.

4. If you want, press on the UniMotion pop-up menu and choose one of the other options for the other Parent texture.

5. The Offspring texture will now show the effects of both motions.

Changing the UniMotion speed

1. If you want a UniMotion to move faster or slower, place your mouse inside the window of the Parent texture. You will see a four-headed arrow.

2. Press and drag quickly to increase the intensity of the UniMotion. Drag slowly to decrease the intensity of the UniMotion (**Figure 12**).

Animated Images
UniMotion options; UniMotion speed

Under the Offspring Preview window is the Blending triangle. Pressing on this displays the controls for the amount of blending between the Parent textures.

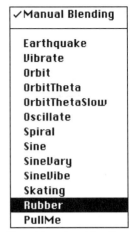

Manual Blending

1. Set the Manual Scooting under the Mother panel so the image in the Mother panel moves from left to right.

2. Set the Manual Scooting under the Father panel so the image in the Father panel moves from top to bottom.

3. Set the Offspring Blending option to Manual blending.

6. The amount of blending, as seen in the Info Area, controls how much influence each Parent texture has.

Figure 13. *The* ***UniMotion Blending*** *menu allows you to set the amount of blending between the* ***Parent*** *textures.*

Manual Blending is static. However, by using any of the UniMotion Blending settings, you can vary the influence between the Parent textures.

An easy way of understanding UniMotion Blending is to think of the editor in a TV studio fading between two cameras. One camera may be moving side to side, the other up and down. However, the editor can fade between the two cameras quickly, slowly, or in certain patterns. The patterns of those fades are the UniMotion Blending.

Adding UniMotion Blending

1. Use the steps above to create an Offspring texture.

2. Change the UniMotion Blending option (**Figure 13**) to Rubber.

3. Notice how the amount of influence of each of the Parent textures changes. This is independent of their motions.

Animated Images
Manual Blending; UniMotion Blending

Figure 14. *The **Frame panels** allow you to store the Offspring images that will be used as the basis of the Interform animation.*

Once you have a texture in motion, the Frame panels can record its settings. These frames are the basis for your animation.

Filling the Frame panels

1. Once you have an Offspring animation you like, click on one of the ten black Frame panels at the bottom of the Interform window (**Figure 14**). The filled frame will show a preview of the texture.

2. Continue to create other Offspring animations until you have as many frames as you want.

Tip

◆ When you create a movie, all of the frames you have saved will be included in the final movie.

Before you can record your animation, you will need to set the Movie Options.

Setting the Movie Options

1. Press on the white triangle to the right of Frame panel 10. This displays the Movie Options menu (**Figure 15**).

2. To set the screen size of your move, choose from 160x120 or 320x240 or 640x480. These are the sizes, in pixels, of the QuickTime screen. If you choose Size of Selection, your animation will take the size of the file you opened in the host application.

3. To set the transition from one frame panel to another, press again on the Movie Options pop-up menu. Choose No Fade to make a sharp cut between the panels. Choose Quick Fade for a fade that is a short amount of time. Choose Slow Fade for a longer fade.

4. To set the length of time each frame panel appears in the animation, press again on the Movie Options pop-up menu. Choose 1 second, 2 seconds, 5 seconds or 10 seconds.

5. To see the preview of your animation in an unending loop, where the end fades into the beginning, press on the Movie Options pop-up menu. Set the option for Loop Movie.

6. To see a preview of your movie press on the Movie Options pop-up menu and choose Preview Movie. You can stop the preview by clicking with the mouse.

```
┌──────────────────────────┐
│  Preview movie           │
│ ✓Loop movie              │
├──────────────────────────┤
│  160 x 120               │
│  320 x 240               │
│  640 x 480               │
│ ✓Size of Selection       │
├──────────────────────────┤
│ ✓No Fade                 │
│  Quick Fade              │
│  Slow Fade               │
├──────────────────────────┤
│  1 second                │
│  2 seconds               │
│  5 seconds               │
│ ✓10 seconds              │
└──────────────────────────┘
```

Figure 15. *The **Movie Options** pop-up menu.*

Movie Options

Figure 16. *The **Record Keyframes button** combines all the frame panels into a QuickTime movie.*

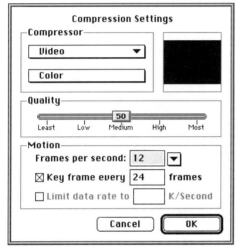

Figure 17. *The **QuickTime Compression Settings** dialog box.*

Once you have set all the movie options, you will want to save your movie into the QuickTime format.

Recording a movie

1. To turn your frame panels into a QuickTime movie, click on the Record Keyframes button (**Figure 16**).

2. Fill out the Save dialog box with the name of your movie and select where you would like to store the movie.

3. Another dialog box will then appear with the Compression settings for your QuickTime movie (**Figure 17**). If you are working with a specific QuickTime application such as Adobe Premiere, consult with the manuals for that program as to the best settings.

4. For most purposes though, the default settings will be fine. Click the OK button. Your Interform frames have been turned into a QuickTime animation.

COMPACT FILTERS 8

The Compact Filters are named and grouped by their common interface, which takes up less room compared to the first four filters. In addition, while each filter creates quite different effects, their controls are quite similar.

Unlike the first four filters which can work with completely blank files, most of these filters need some sort of underlying image for their effects to be noticeable. This can be a simple scan, a photograph, or plain brush strokes. However, as the artwork on the facing page shows, it is possible to create complete illustrations without using any images except those created by the Compact Filters.

In this chapter you will learn

◆ The Glass Lens filter.

◆ The Page Curl filter.

◆ The Planar Tile filter.

◆ The Seamless Welder filter.

◆ The Twirl filter.

◆ The Video Feedback filter.

◆ The Vortex Tile filter.

◆ The 3D Stereo Noise filter.

Compact Filters

GLASS LENS

As you saw in Chapter 4, the Spheroid Designer can be used to create transparent glass spheres. However, you do have to change many of the settings for opacity, color, etc. If all you want is a plain glass sphere, the Glass Lens filter is much faster and easier.

Making a selection for the Glass Lens

1. With the host application open, open a file that contains some sort of image. If your file doesn't have some sort of image your glass lens will look more like a solid sphere.

2. To make a circular lens, make a square selection over the portion of the image you would like to have the lens on (**Figure 1**). If you want the lens to fill the entire image, make no selection.

3. To make a lens that is elliptical, make a rectangular or elliptical selection over your image.

4. Choose KPT Glass Lens 3.0 from the KPT 3.0 menu. This will open the Glass Lens filter (**Figure 2**).

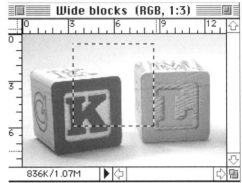

Figure 1. *Make a selection over the area where you would like to have your lens.*

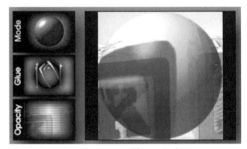

Figure 2. *The **Glass Lens** filter window.*

Glass Lens

Figure 3. *Pressing on the **Mode** pop-up menu displays the lighting choices: **Soft**, **Normal**, or **Bright**.*

Figure 4. *The results of applying the **Glass Lens** filter to an image.*

Creating a Glass Lens

1. With the filter active, press on the Mode Control panel pop-up menu to choose from Soft, Normal or Bright light for your lens (**Figure 3**).

2. Press on the Opacity Control panel and drag to the left to decrease the opacity of your lens. (A real glass lens will not just distort the image, but will let some of the undistorted image show through.)

3. Press and drag on the image in the Preview window to change the direction of the light shining on the lens.

4. Click the OK button to apply the filter to your image (**Figure 4**).

Tips

◆ Choose Black Background from the Options pop-up menu to surround your lens with black rather than the original image.

◆ Choose Toggle Backlight to direct the light onto the back of your lens.

◆ In addition to working with the Opacity Control panel, see Chapter 12, "Apply Modes" for other ways to have your image interact with the lens.

Glass Lens

PAGE CURL

While this filter may have become a bit overused (especially in computer catalogs) it does offer the quickest and easiest way to create what otherwise would be an extremely difficult effect.

Creating a Page Curl

1. With the host application open, open a file that contains some sort of image. If your file doesn't have some sort of image your page curl will be turning empty pages.

2. Choose KPT Page Curl 3.0 from the KPT 3.0 menu. This will open the Page Curl filter (**Figure 5**).

3. Press on any one of the eight arrows around the Preview window. They control the corner and direction of the curl.

4. Drag in the direction of the arrow to increase the depth of the curl.

5. Press on the Mode Control panel pop-up menu to choose the color of the page that is being shown as the page curls up (**Figure 6**).

Figure 5. *The Page Curl filter window.*

Figure 6. *The Mode Control panel pop-up menu lets you choose the foreground or background color of the host application to apply to the page being revealed by the curl.*

Page Curl

Figure 7. *Press and drag to the left or right on the* ***Opacity Control panel*** *to change the opacity of the page being curled.*

Figure 8. *Press and drag to the left or right on the* ***Page Opacity Control*** *(circled) to change the opacity page being revealed.*

Figure 9. *Two curls applied to the same image. The top curl used no transparency on the curl or the page being revealed. The bottom curl used a transparency on both the curl and the page being revealed.*

Once you've created an ordinary page curl, you can then change the default settings to create a transparent page curl, such as a piece of film.

Creating a transparent Page Curl

1. Press on the Opacity Control panel (**Figure 7**) and drag to the left to decrease the opacity of the page being curled. This creates the effect of the curled page being a piece of film.

2. Press and drag on the small Opacity square located at the bottom left corner of the preview window (**Figure 8**). This controls the amount of opacity of the image onto the page being revealed.

3. Click the OK button to apply the filter to your image (**Figure 9**).

Tips

◆ While you can only apply one page curl at a time, you can create multiple curls by reapplying the filter at different corners.

◆ In addition to working with the Opacity Control panel, see Chapter 12, "Apply Modes" for other ways to have your image interact with the curl.

Transparent Page Curl

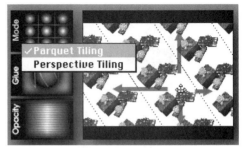

PLANAR TILE

This is the filter to create infinite ground planes. You have a choice of Parquet Tiling or Perspective Tiling.

Creating a tiled plane

1. With the host application open, open a file that contains some sort of image. If the file doesn't have an image the filter will not appear to work.

2. Choose KPT Planar Tile 3.0 from the KPT 3.0 menu. This will open the Planar Tile filter (**Figure 10**).

3. Press on the Mode Control panel pop-up menu to choose Parquet or Perspective Tiling.

4. Press on the Opacity Control panel and drag to the left to decrease the opacity of the tiles being created. (This will allow the original image to show through.)

5. Position the four-headed arrow inside the Preview window and drag to the left or right to rotate the tiles within the window. In Perspective Mode, this skews the plane from side to side.

6. Position the four-headed arrow inside the Preview window and drag up or down to increase or decrease the size of the tiles. In Perspective Mode, this raises or lowers the horizon.

7. Click the OK button to apply the filter to your image (**Figure 11**).

Tip

◆ In addition to working with the Opacity Control panel, see Chapter 12, "Apply Modes" for other ways to have your image interact with the tiles.

Figure 10. *Press on the **Mode Control panel** to choose between **Parquet Tiling** and **Perspective Tiling**.*

Figure 11. *The **Planar Tile** filter was applied to the complete image of the car creating the perspective tile effect. A silhouetted image of the car was then pasted onto the tiles.*

Planar Tile

Figure 12. *The difference between an ordinary image used to define a pattern (top) and an image that has had the Seamless Welder applied (bottom). Notice the sharp line in the ordinary image.*

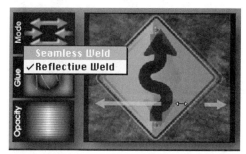

Figure 13. *The Seamless Welder filter window.*

SEAMLESS WELDER

Once you have applied the Seamless Welder to an image, it can be used to define a pattern with no edge (**Figure 12**).

Using the Seamless Welder

1. Open a file that contains an image. If you want a certain part of the image to become the pattern, make a selection around that part of the image.

2. Choose KPT Seamless Welder 3.0 from the KPT 3.0 menu. (If you get a notice about the size of the selection, see the tips at the bottom of this page.)

3. You should now see the Seamless Welder filter (**Figure 13**).

4. Press on the Mode Control pop-up menu to choose between Seamless Weld and Reflective Weld.

5. Press on the Opacity Control panel and drag to the left to decrease the opacity of the tiles being created.

6. Position the two-headed arrow inside the Preview window and drag to the left to decrease the intensity of the filter. Drag to the right to increase the intensity.

7. Click the OK button to apply the filter to your image.

8. In Photoshop, select the entire image and choose Define Pattern from the Edit menu to complete the process.

Tips

◆ The Seamless Welder uses information from outside the selection. If you have no selection, or too large a selection within the image, you will see a notice telling you the results of the filter may not be satisfactory.

◆ If you get this notice, use the Reflective Welder setting which uses information from within the selection.

TWIRL

This filter has two different mode settings. Twirl distorts the image as if in a whirlpool. Kaleidoscope distorts the image as if in a...(you get the idea).

Using the Twirl mode

1. With the host application open, open a file that contains some sort of image.

2. Choose KPT Twirl 3.0 from the KPT 3.0 menu.

3. Press on the Mode Control panel pop-up menu to choose Twirl (**Figure 14**).

4. Position the two-headed arrow inside the Preview window and drag to the left or right to change the direction and intensity. Click the OK button to apply the filter to your image (**Figure 15**).

Using the Kaleidoscope mode

1. With the Twirl filter open, press on the Mode Control panel pop-up menu to choose Kaleidascope (**Figure 16**).

2. Position the four-headed arrow inside the Preview window.

3. Drag up to increase the number of segments of the kaleidoscope image. Drag down to decrease the number.

4. Drag to the left or right to change the angle of the segments. Click the OK button to apply the filter to your image (**Figure 17**).

Tips

◆ When dragging in the Preview window, you can constrain your movement to vertical by holding the Option key.

◆ You can constrain your movement to horizontal by holding the Control key.

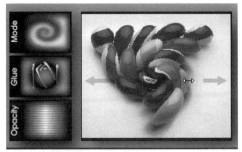

Figure 14. *The* **Twirl** *filter window.*

Figure 15. *The results of applying the* **Twirl** *filter to an image.*

Figure 16. *The* **Kaleidoscope** *filter window.*

Figure 17. *The results of applying the* **Kaleido-scope** *filter to an image.*

Twirl

Figure 18. *The Video Feedback filter window.*

Figure 19. *The results of applying the Video Feedback filter to an image.*

VIDEO FEEDBACK

Have you ever seen a television camera focused on a monitor that shows a picture of the monitor showing a picture of the monitor showing a picture…? Well, that's the idea behind the Video Feedback filter. Video Feedback has two modes: Video Feedback and Telescopic Feedback.

Using the Video Feedback mode

1. With the host application open, open a file that contains some sort of image.

2. Choose KPT Video Feedback 3.0 from the KPT 3.0 menu. You should now see the Video Feedback filter (**Figure 18**).

3. Press on the Mode Control panel pop-up menu to choose between Video Feedback or Telescopic Feedback.

4. If you want, press on the Opacity Control panel and drag to the left to decrease the opacity of the tiles being created. (This will allow the original image to show through.)

5. Drag inside the Preview window to change the end point of the feedback loop.

6. Position the two-headed arrow over the Feedback Intensity Control and drag to the right to increase intensity which will increase the number of repitions. Drag to the left to decrease the intensity which will decrease the number of repitions.

7. Drag left or right on the Angle Control to adjust the direction and degree of rotation of successive images.

8. Click the OK button to apply the filter to your image (**Figure 19**).

Tip

◆ The Telescopic Feedback mode changes the repeated image from a rectangle to an ellipse.

Video Feedback

VORTEX TILE

The Vortex Tile filter is similar to the effect of a kaleidoscope. But instead of triangular slices, this kaleidoscope repeats in circular patterns. (It's a lot easier to create the effect than it is to describe.)

Using the Vortex Tile filter

1. With the host application open, open a file that contains some sort of image.

2. Choose KPT Vortext Tile 3.0 from the KPT 3.0 menu.

3. You should now see the Vortex Tile filter (**Figure 20**).

3. Press on the Mode Control panel pop-up menu to choose between Normal Vortex or Pinch Vortex.

4. If you want, press on the Opacity Control panel and drag to the left to decrease the opacity of the tiles being created. (This will allow the original image to show through.)

5. Drag inside the Preview window to change the focal point of the vortex.

6. Position the two-headed arrow over the Vortex Radius control. Drag to the right to increase intensity. Drag to the left to decrease the intensity.

7. Click the OK button to apply the filter to your image (**Figure 21**).

Tip

◆ The Pinch Vortex causes the image to appear to fold into itself.

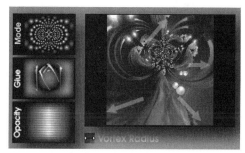

Figure 20. *The **Vortex Tile** filter window.*

Figure 21. *The results of applying the **Vortex Tile** filter to an image.*

Figure 22. *The 3D Stereo Noise filter window.*

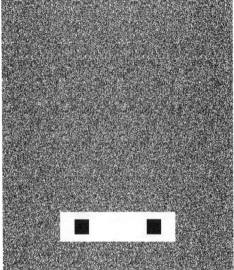

Figure 23. *The results of applying the 3D Stereo Noise filter to an image. If you can unfocus your eyes as you stare at the image, you should be able to see a 3D image of a pair of justice scales.*

3D STEREO NOISE

This is a filter that creates those strange images where if you allow your eyes to unfocus you can see a 3D effect. Some people have no problem seeing the image. Others (like this author) have never been able to see the effect. Oh well, here's the filter that can create the look.

Using the 3D Stereo Noise filter

1. With the host application open, open a file that contains some sort of image. Convert the image to grayscale and blur slightly.

2. Choose KPT 3D Stereo Noise 3.0 from the KPT 3.0 menu.

3. You should now see the 3D Stereo Noise filter (**Figure 22**).

4. Press on the Mode Control panel pop-up menu to choose between Monochrome Noise, Color Noise or No Noise.

5. If you want, press on the Opacity Control panel and drag to the left to decrease the opacity of the tiles being created. (This will allow the original image to show through.)

6. Drag inside the Preview window to the right to increase the intensity of the noise effect. Drag to the left to descrease the intensity.

7. Press on the options triangle in the upper right corner to show or hide the focus dots.

8. Click the OK button to apply the filter to your image (**Figure 23**).

Tip

◆ If you are having trouble seeing the images try focusing on an object across the room and then bring the 3D Stereo Noise image into view.

3D Stereo Noise

After you have made one sphere, you may want to create many spheres at once. This is where you can use the Apply Bubbles.

Creating multiple spheres that you like ... of that sphere pattern

1. Once your ... spheres, click on the you can ... spheres ... using the ... that is fifth from the

2. ... on the small white triangle ... the Apply bubbles to view the ... Menu. These are the options as ... your spheres will be arranged (**Figure 26**).

... a random arrangement of ... and position where your spheres ... not overlap, choose Apollonian ... To create a random ... of size and position where ... spheres will overlap, choose ... spheres (**Figure 27**).

Tips

◆ Ap... Star ... Radial ... patterns ... Spiral Packing ... are chosen us... Packing and

◆ If you choose the "..." ... option, your spheres will ... their ... onto their background.

◆ If you choose the "Use Mutation" option, multiple spheres will appear with random mutations based on the settings in the Mutation Tree (see following page).

◆ For illustrations of the various patterns of the Apply Menu, see Appendix XXX.

Apollonian Packing
Random Spheres
Random Ellipses

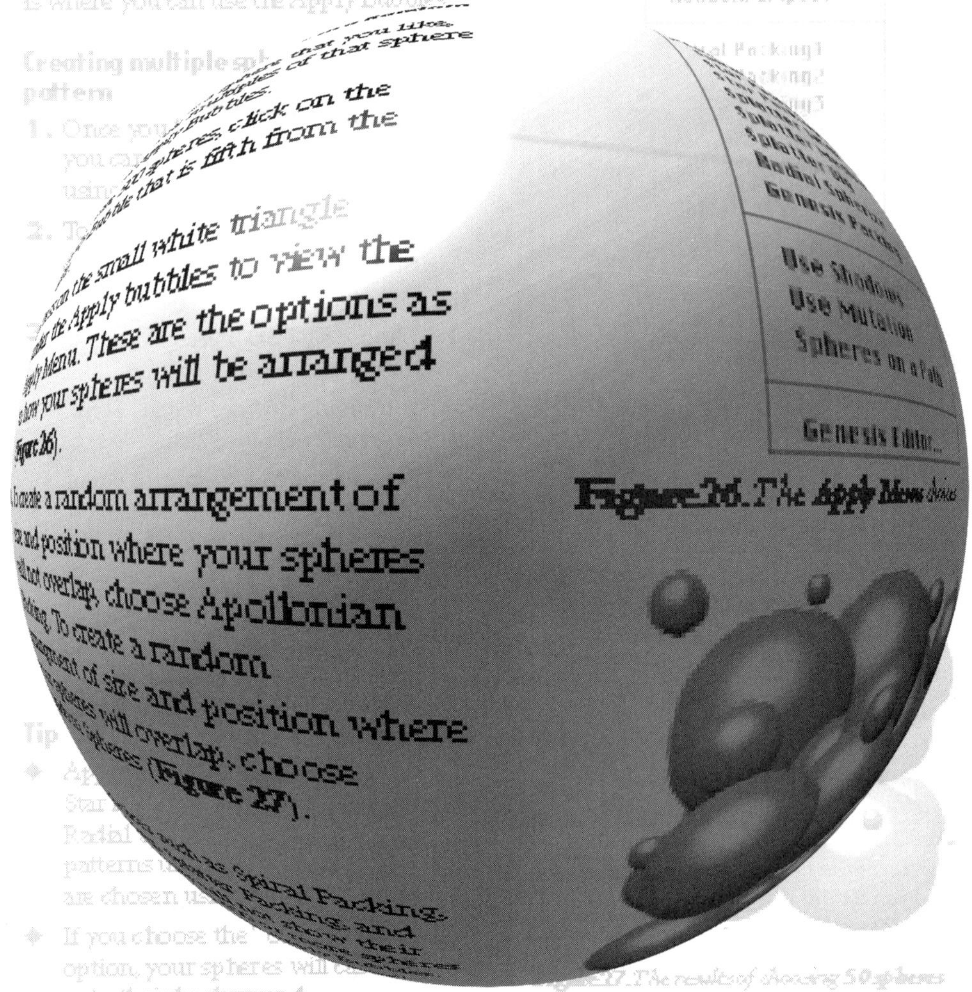

...al Packing1
... Packing2
... Packing3
Spiral ...
Spiral ...
Radial ...
Genesis Packing

Use Shadows
Use Mutation
Spheres on a Path

Genesis Editor...

Figure 26. The **Apply** Menu ...

Figure 27. The results of choosing 50 spheres arranged using the **Random Spheres** setting.

LENS f/x FILTERS 9

All of the Lens f/x filters have the same interface that resembles a camera lens. They are probably the easiest of the Kai's Power Tools to master. Many of the filters have equivalents in applications such as Photoshop. But the Lens f/x filters have variations that make them unique.

In this chapter you will learn how to use each of the six filters: Pixel, Gaussian. Edge, Intensity, Smudge, and Noise. You will also learn about a seventh bonus filter called MetaToys that has Glass Lens and Twirl filters.

Tips

◆ Each of the Lens f/x filters can be moved anywhere around your screen. This means you can see how the filters look over the menu bars, tool palette, even the trash can. However, the effect of the filters will only be applied to the image in the host application.

◆ You can still see a preview of your image, no matter where the lens is located. Just click on the preview button at the top of the lens interface.

◆ If you are in one of the lens filters, you can switch to another by pressing on the small white triangle under the words KPT Lens f/x.

PIXEL f/x

This filter creates the effect of turning the pixels in your image into grains of sand. These grains can then be blown, scattered, or tossed.

Using the Pixel f/x filter

1. With the host application open, open a file that contains some sort of image.

2. Choose KPT Pixel f/x 3.0 from the KPT 3.0 menu.

3. Drag the Lens f/x control so that the lens is over the area of the image you would like to preview (**Figure 1**).

4. To change the type of effect, press on the Mode Gauge at the bottom of the lens to choose from Diffuse More, PixelWeather 1 and Pixel Weather 2 pop-up menu (**Figure 1**).

5. To change how many directions the effect is applied to, press on the Options Gauge at the top of the lens to choose from Unidirectional (one direction), Bidirectional (along an axis), or Omnidirectional (every which way) (**Figure 1**).

6. If you choose Unidirectional or Bidirectional, a Direction Control Ball will appear around the rim of the preview window. Drag this to set the actual direction.

7. Drag on the Intensity Control ball on the outside left of the lens to increase or decrease the effect (**Figure 2**).

8. Drag on the Opacity Control Ball next to the Intensity Control Ball to allow more of the original image to be seen. (See Chapter 12, "Apply Modes" for other ways to have your image interact with the filter.)

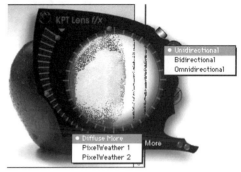

Figure 1. *The Pixel f/x lens.*

Figure 2. *The effect of the Pixel f/x filter applied to the right side of the image.*

Pixel f/x

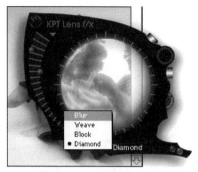

Figure 3. *The Gaussian f/x lens.*

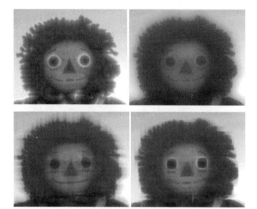

Figure 4. *The four effects of the Gaussian f/x filter: (clockwise from top right)* **Blur, Weave, Block,** *and* **Diamond.**

GAUSSIAN f/x

Gaussian blurs are blurs with a slight glowing effect. The Gaussian f/x filter lets you create Gaussian blurs, Gaussian weaves, blocks and diamonds.

Using the Gaussian f/x filter

1. With the host application open, open a file that contains some sort of image.

2. Choose KPT Gaussian f/x 3.0 from the KPT 3.0 menu.

3. Drag the Lens f/x control so that the lens is over the area of the image you would like to preview (**Figure 3**).

4. To change the type of effect, press on the Mode Gauge at the bottom of the lens to choose from Blur, Weave, Block or Diamond.

5. Drag on the Intensity Control Ball on the outside left of the lens to increase or decrease the effect (**Figure 4**).

6. Drag on the Opacity Control Ball next to the Intensity Control Ball to allow more of the original image to be seen. (See Chapter 12, "Apply Modes" for other ways to have your image interact with the filter.)

Gaussian f/x

EDGE f/x

In general, Edge filters, such as those found in Photoshop, look for the differences between pixel values and then create an outline at that point. The KPT Edge f/x filter gives you more variations over the types of edging.

Tip

◆ The Edge f/x filters will create an image that looks like a negative of the original. Use the Invert command in the host application to create a positive effect.

Using the Edge f/x filter

1. With the host application open, open a file that contains some sort of image.

2. Choose KPT Edge f/x 3.0 from the KPT 3.0 menu.

3. Drag the Lens f/x control so that the lens is over the area of the image you would like to preview (**Figure 5**).

4. To change the type of effect, press on the Mode Gauge at the bottom of the lens to choose from Normal, Soft, or Directional.

5. If you have chosen Directional, drag on the Direction Control Ball at the edge of the Preview window to change the direction.

6. Drag on the Intensity Control Ball on the outside left of the lens to increase or decrease the effect (**Figure 6**).

7. Drag on the Opacity Control Ball next to the Intensity Control Ball to allow more of the original image to be seen. (See Chapter 12, "Apply Modes" for other ways to have your image interact with the filter.)

Figure 5. *The Edge f/x lens.*

Figure 6. *The three modes of the Edge f/x filter: (from top to bottom)* **Normal, Soft,** *and* **Directional.** *(The Invert command was applied in the host application to create a positive effect.)*

Edge f/x

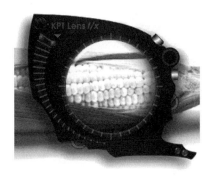

Figure 7. *The **Intensity f/x** lens.*

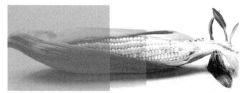

Figure 8. *Different looks of the **Intensity f/x** filter: (left to right) 25%, 50%, and 100% Intensity.*

INTENSITY f/x

The Intensity f/x filter changes the saturation and intensity of the colors in an image.

Using the Intensity f/x filter

1. With the host application open, open a file that contains some sort of image.

2. Choose KPT Intensity f/x 3.0 from the KPT 3.0 menu.

3. Drag the Lens f/x control so that the lens is over the area of the image you would like to preview (**Figure 7**).

4. Drag on the Intensity Control Ball on the outside left of the lens to increase or decrease the effect (**Figure 8**). Numbers above 50% will increase the saturation of the colors. Numbers below 50% will decrease the saturation.

5. If you want, drag on the Opacity Control Ball next to the Intensity Control Ball to allow more of the original image to be seen. (See Chapter 12, "Apply Modes" for other ways to have your image interact with the filter.)

SMUDGE f/x

The Smudge f/x filter uses a combination of blur and blend to create a smudge effect. The Smudge f/x filter has two modes: Smudge and Drip.

Using the Smudge f/x filter

1. With the host application open, open a file that contains some sort of image.

2. Choose KPT Smudge f/x 3.0 from the KPT 3.0 menu.

3. Drag the Lens f/x control so that the lens is over the area of the image you would like to preview (**Figure 9**).

4. Press on the Mode Gauge at the bottom of the lens to choose between Smudge and Drip.

5. If you have chosen Drip, press on the Options Gauge (located between the two silver knobs at the top of the lens) to access the Color Wheel. Drag the eyedropper on the wheel or the original image to choose the color that you want to drip.

6. Drag on the Intensity Control Ball on the outside left of the lens to increase the effect (**Figure 10**).

7. Drag on the Direction Control Ball at the edge of the Preview window to change the direction of the effect.

8. To combine the Smudge with the original image, drag on the Opacity Control Ball next to the Intensity Control Ball. (See Chapter 12, "Apply Modes" for other ways to have your image interact with the filter.)

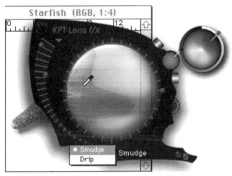

Figure 9. *The Smudge f/x lens.*

Figure 10. *The Smudge f/x filter: in the **Smudge mode** (top) and **Drip mode** (bottom). (The Opacity level was lowered to let more of the image to show through the Smudge mode.)*

Smudge f/x

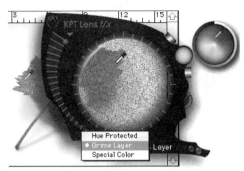

Figure 11. *The Noise f/x lens.*

Figure 12. *The effects of the Noise f/x filter: (from top to bottom)* **Original image, Hue Protected, Grime Layer, Special Color.**

NOISE f/x

The Noise f/x filter lets you add a random dithered pattern to create textures and effects.

Using the Noise f/x filter

1. With the host application open, open a file that contains some sort of image.

2. Choose KPT Noise f/x 3.0 from the KPT 3.0 menu.

3. Drag the Lens f/x control so that the lens is over the area of the image you would like to preview (**Figure 11**).

4. Press on the Mode Gauge at the bottom of the lens to choose the type of noise.

5. Choose Hue Protected to create noise that comes from the original colors of your image. Choose Grime Layer to add a strong dark color of noise. Choose Special Color to add noise that is a certain color (**Figure 12**).

6. If you have chosen Special Color, press on the Options Gauge (located between the two silver knobs at the top of the lens) to access the Color Wheel. Drag the eyedropper on the wheel or the original image to choose the color that you want to use as your noise.

7. Drag on the Intensity Control Ball on the outside left of the lens to increase the effect.

8. If you want, drag on the Opacity Control Ball next to the Intensity Control Ball to allow more of the original image to be seen. (See Chapter 12, "Apply Modes" for other ways to have your image interact with the filter.)

Noise f/x

METATOYS f/x

The MetaToys f/x contains versions of the Glass Lens and Twirl filters described in the Compact Filters chapter. The MetaToys versions of those filters are very similar. However, they do allow you do move the lens interface over any area of your screen.

This means you can see what it would be like to make a glass lens of your desktop or twirl the trash can. Unfortunately, the MetaToys will only distort the elements of an image, not any of the screen elements. That's why they are called toys.

Using the Glass Lens f/x filter

1. Choose KPT MetaToys f/x 3.0 from the KPT 3.0 menu. Press on the Options triangle in the upper left area of the lens to choose the Glass Lens option.

2. Position the MetaToys lens over the area of the image you want to distort or the area of the screen you want to preview (**Figure 13**).

3. Press the Mode Gauge to choose Soft, Normal or Bright lighting.

4. Press on the Options Gauge to choose Front Light or Back Light.

5. Drag on the Direction Control Ball at the edge of the Preview window to change the direction of the light.

6. Drag on the Opacity Control Ball next to the Intensity Control Ball to allow more of the original image to be seen. (See Chapter 12, "Apply Modes" for other ways to have your image interact with the filter.)

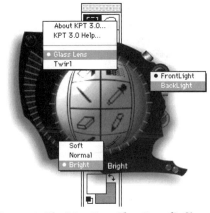

Figure 13. *The MetaToys Glass Lens f/x filter can be positioned over onscreen elements but will only distort elements in an image.*

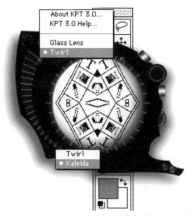

Figure 14. *The MetaToys Twirl f/x filter in the Kaleida mode. The filter can be positioned over onscreen elements but will only distort elements in an image.*

Using the Twirl f/x filter

1. Choose KPT MetaToys f/x 3.0 from the KPT 3.0 menu. Press on the Options triangle in the upper left area of the lens to choose the Twirl option.

2. Position the MetaToys lens over the area of the image you want to distort or the area of the screen you want to preview (**Figure 14**).

3. Press on the Mode Gauge to choose Twirl or Kaleida.

4. Drag on the Direction Control Ball at the edge of the Preview window to change the direction and intensity of the twirl or the direction of the kaleida slices.

5. Drag on the Intensity Control Ball to increase the number of slices.

6. If you want, drag on the Opacity Control Ball next to the Intensity Control Ball to allow more of the original image to be seen. (See Chapter 12, "Apply Modes" for other ways to have your image interact with the filter.)

TEXTURE EXPLORER 2.1

U sually when a program has a new version, the older version is quietly retired to the sidelines. However, unlike the textures created with Texture Explorer 3.0, the textures created with Texture Explorer 2.1 are repeating textures (**Figure 1**). That means that you can use these textures as the basis of backgrounds for multimedia, web designs, bump maps, and other applications that need a repeating tile. Also, the Texture Explorer 3.0 cannot use presets created for the previous versions. So if you have presets for 2.1, you will need to keep using that version. Therefore MetaTools ships the Texture Explorer 2.1 along with 3.0. While you will probably want to use the current version for most of your work, you can use the previous version when necessary.

In this chapter you will learn
- ◆ Launching the Texture Explorer through the host application.
- ◆ Clearing the settings.
- ◆ Using the Preview window.
- ◆ Controlling Mutations.
- ◆ Using the Shuffle button.
- ◆ Using the Color Globe.
- ◆ Using the Gradient Bar.
- ◆ Moving the Source Texture.
- ◆ Using the Transparency Options.
- ◆ Applying a Global Transparency.
- ◆ Selecting the Tile size.
- ◆ Using Texture Protection.
- ◆ Using the Add Preset button and Presets menu.
- ◆ Using the Preset keyboard shortcuts.

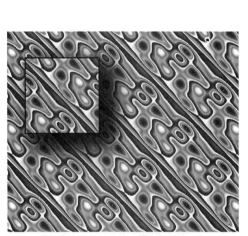

Figure 1. *How a texture created in* **Texture Explorer 2.1** *can be* **tiled** *to create patterns.*

Preparing to make a texture

1. With the host application open, start with a blank file.

2. Choose KPT Texture Explorer 2.1 from the KPT 2.1 menu.

3. You will now work inside the Texture Explorer 2.1 (**Figure 2**).

Changing the Source Texture

1. Once you launch the Texture Explorer, you already have a Source Texture available in the Preview window.

2. Click on one of the Derivative Texture windows located around the Source Texture window. That Derivative Texture will take the place of the original Source Texture. And new Derivative Textures will be created.

Using the Preview window

1. Click on the Preview window to see a representation of the texture as it will appear in your file.

2. Click again on the Preview window to go back to the Texture Explorer.

The Derivative Textures are mutations of the Source Texture.

Controlling the mutations

1. Move your mouse across the Mutation Tree. As you pass over each of the balls they will change color from red to cyan or back to red. The more red balls the greater the mutations of the Derivative Textures will be.

2. Move your mouse over the lowest red ball.

3. Click on the red ball. You will see that the Derivative Textures are much closer to the Source Texture (**Figure 3**).

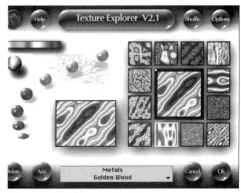

Figure 2. *The **Texture Explorer 2.1**.*

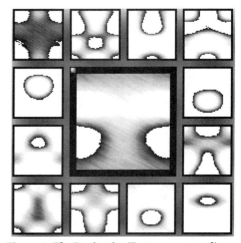

Figure 3. *The **Derivative Textures** surrounding a **Source Texture** where the **Mutation Tree** has been set for **Minimum Mutation**.*

Source Texture; Preview window; Controlling mutations

All Parameters
None

✓**Colors**
✓**Apply Mode**
✓**Test Image**
✓**Feature Size**
✓**Rotation**
✓**Distortion**
✓**Random Seed**

Figure 4. *Press on the **Shuffle button** to see the **Mutation Options** pop-up menu.*

Figure 5. *Click on the **Color Globe** to change just the colors of your texture.*

Using the Shuffle button

1. Press on the Shuffle button at the top of the Texture Explorer. You will see a pop-up menu with the options for your mutations (**Figure 4**).

2. Choose which attributes of the texture you want to have affected by the Shuffle button.

3. Each time you click on the button, the Derivative Textures will mutate according to the attributes you selected.

Tip

◆ The setting for the Mutation Tree does not affect the action of the Shuffle button.

Once you have a texture pattern that you like, you can choose to mutate only its colors using the Color Globe.

Using the Color Globe

1. Fill the Preview window with the Source Texture that you like.

2. Instead of clicking on the Mutation Tree, click on the Color Globe to the right of the Mutation Tree (**Figure 5**).

3. Each time you click only the colors of the Derivative Textures will change. The basic shape, size, angle, etc. of the texture will remain the same.

4. Continue to click on the Color Globe to change the colors of the Derivative Textures.

Tip

◆ Clicking the Color Globe creates the same effect as using the Shuffle button with just the Colors option active.

Instead of relying on the mutations of the Color Globe to find the gradient you like, you can also access the stored gradients through the Gradient Bar.

Using the Gradient Bar

1. Press on the Gradient Bar. You will see a pop-up menu containing a list of all the presets from the Gradient Designer (**Figure 6**).

2. Choose the gradient you would like to apply to your texture.

3. This will apply that gradient to your pattern without changing any of the other attributes.

You can also move the Source Texture to see more of the texture.

Moving the Source Texture

1. Position your mouse inside the Realtime Preview window which is located to the left of the Derivative Textures.

2. Press and drag to move the Source Texture (**Figure 7**).

Tip

◆ If you have clicked in the Preview window to see your texture, you can still use the Realtime Preview window to see the position of your texture.

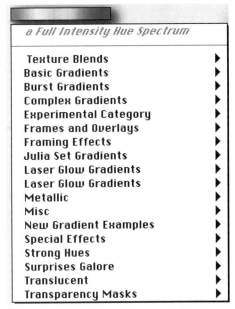

Figure 6. *Press on the **Gradient Bar** below the **Color Globe** to see a pop-up menu of all the available **Gradient Presets**.*

Figure 7. *Press and drag in the **Realtime Preview** window to reposition your texture.*

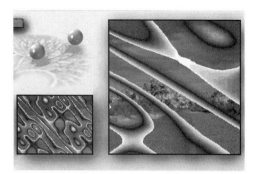

*Figure 8. The **Preview window** shows the effects of applying a transparent texture to an image.*

If the gradient for your textures contains opaque areas, you can turn the transparency for those areas on or off.

Using the Transparency Option

1. To best understand the effects of the Transparency Option, open a file that contains some sort of image.

2. Press on the Options button and choose Use Current Selection from the bottom part of the menu.

3. Press again on the Options button and choose Use Transparency from the very bottom of the menu.

4. Depending on the current gradient, you may or may not see the original image.

5. Press on the Gradient Bar and choose choose one of the textures listed in the Translucent category. You will now see your original image in the transparent areas of the gradient (**Figure 8**).

Tip

◆ For other ways to have your image interact with the texture, see Chapter 12, "Apply Modes."

*Figure 9. The effect of pressing the number key 5 to apply a **50% transparency** to the texture that was applied over the right side of the image.*

Even if there are no transparent areas in your gradient, you can still apply a transparency to the entire texture.

Applying a Global Transparency

1. Hold one of the number keys when clicking the OK button to change the transparency of the texture that is being created (**Figure 9**).

2. Press on the number 1 key to apply the texture at just 10%.

3. Each of the other numbers 2–0 correspond to 20%–100%.

You can also change the size of the final texture to a specific size or selection size.

Selecting the Tile Size

1. Press on the Preview window to see the menu of the tile size options.
2. Choose Tile Size of Selection to fill your selection without any repetitions.
3. Choose one of the numerical tile sizes to fill your file (**Figure 10**).

Tips

◆ If the tile is larger than the selection, then part of the texture will be visible.

◆ Click on the Preview window to preview which area of the texture will be visible.

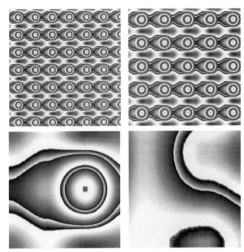

Figure 10. *How changing the tile size affects the finished texture. From top to bottom:* **Tile 96, Tile 128, Tile Size of Selection, Tile 1024.**

Once you have a texture that you like, you will want to save its settings. There are two ways to save a setting: Texture Protection and Presets.

Using Texture Protection

1. When you see a Derivative Texture that you like, hold the Option key and click on the window for that Derivative Texture.
2. A red line will appear around the Texture window. This indicates that the texture is protected. Any mutations, or changes you make will not affect that texture (**Figure 11**).
3. Any texture that is protected can be applied to the Source Texture in the usual fashion.
4. To release the protection from a Derivative Texture, hold the Option key as you click on the window. The texture will now change along with the rest of the Derivative Textures.

Figure 11. *A red line around a* **Derivative Texture** *indicates that* **Texture Protection** *has been applied.*

```
Save Texture As...
Preset Hub:  KPT User Presets
Category:    Marble
Name:  My swirling marble
```

Figure 12. *The **Preset menu** displays the name of the currently applied preset.*

Using the Add Preset button

1. Once you have a texture with settings that you want to save, click on the Add Preset button.

2. A dialog box will appear where you can enter the name of your setting (**Figure 12**).

3. When you have named your preset, click OK. This will add your preset to the Preset menu.

The Texture Explorer ships with over 300 built-in presets. These can be accessed through the Preset menu.

Using the Preset menu

1. Press on the small black triangle to the right of the Preset menu. This will show preset category pop-up menu.

2. Choose a category and then the preset. That preset will be applied to your Source Texture.

3. The current preset will be listed in the Preset menu.

Using the Preset Keyboard Shortcuts

The following are the keyboard shortcuts to navigate through the Preset menu.

◆ Next preset, Down Arrow.

◆ Previous preset, Up Arrow.

◆ Next category, Option-Page Down.

◆ Previous category, Option-Page Up.

◆ First category, Option-Home.

◆ Last category, Option-End.

◆ Next gradient, Right Arrow.

◆ Previous gradient, Left Arrow

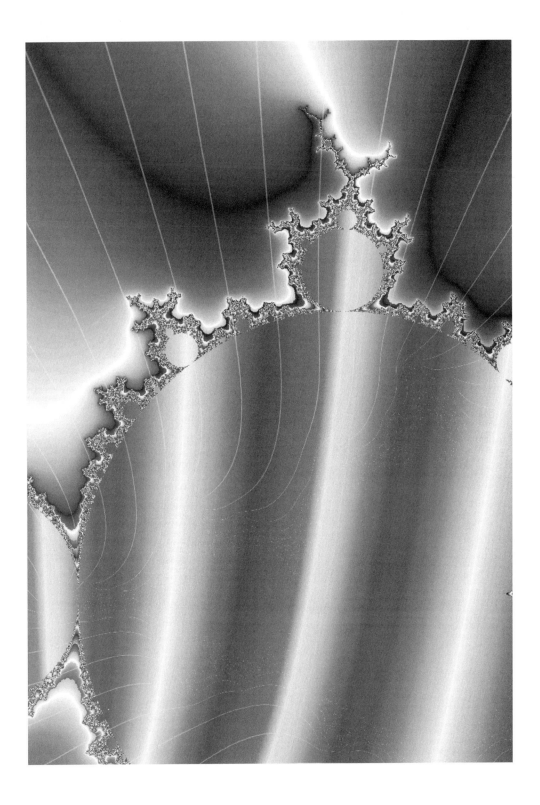

FRACTAL EXPLORER 11

L ike the Texture Explorer 2.0 covered in the previous chapter, the Fractal Explorer was originally released as part of Kai's Power Tools 2.0. It's hard to understand why it was not updated to a 3.0 version. Perhaps they felt it was perfect the way it was. Or not enough people understood fractals. Whatever the reason, the only Fractal Explorer is the older version 2.1.

For those of you who are not familiar with fractals, they are mathematical formulas describing the look of objects. And changing the mathematical formulas will change the look of the objects. Each of the different fractal formulas has been given names.

In this chapter you will learn

◆ Launching the Fractal Explorer through the host application.

◆ Clearing the settings.

◆ Choosing the six fractal design shapes.

◆ Moving around a shape.

◆ Zooming in and out of a design.

◆ Using the Zoom slider.

◆ Changing the Color Outside and Color Inside.

◆ Changing the Loop order.

◆ Using the Wrapping Controls.

◆ Using the Opacity Control panel.

◆ Using the Shuffle button.

◆ Using the Detail Controls.

◆ Storing and opening presets.

Understanding fractals

An easy way to understand fractals is is to imagine that each fractal is the map of a certain area. The land masses in each area have different shapes. However, if you look at one land mass from a airplane, it will look one way. But if you were to zoom in very close on that area, there will be details that you couldn't see before.

For instance, if you look at the Fractal called M-J Hybrid 2 zoomed out, you will see a certain shape. However, if you zoom in on the same fractal, you will see other details (**Figure 1**). Working with fractals is simply a question of knowing which land area has what shape and where you can find interesting details.

Preparing to make a fractal design

1. With the host application open, start with a blank file.

2. Choose KPT Fractal Explorer 2.1 from the KPT 2.1 menu.

3. You will now work inside the Fractal Explorer (**Figure 2**).

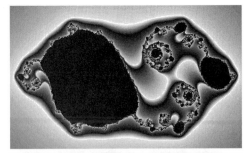
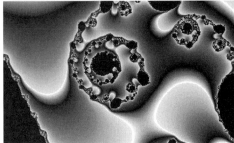

Figure 1. *The difference between an **overview of a fractal** (top) and a **more detailed version of the same fractal** (bottom).*

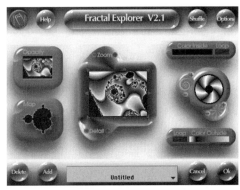

Figure 2. *The **Fractal Explorer 2.1**.*

Figure 3. *The **Color Inside** gradient ramp.*

Figure 4. *The **Color Outside** gradient ramp.*

Figure 5. *The **red circle** of the **Map panel** indicates the position of the view of the fractal design.*

Figure 6. *Clearing the settings will result in a plain fractal image.*

The simplest way to understand fractals is to look first at the six basic fractal shapes. To do so, it is a good idea if you clear some of the colors and other fancy elements of the fractals and just concentrate on the basic shapes.

Clearing the Fractal Explorer

1. Press on the Color Inside gradient ramp (**Figure 3**). This will display the preset gradients for the interior of the fractal design. Choose Solid Black.

2. Press on the Color Outside gradient ramp (**Figure 4**). This will display the preset gradients for the exterior of the fractal design. Choose Solid White.

3. Press on the Map panel to display the menu with the six fractal shapes. Choose Mandelbrot.

4. Hold the Command key and move the small red circle inside the Map panel so that it is in the middle of the black area (**Figure 5**).

5. Press on the Opacity Control panel and choose Use Current Selection from the pop-up menu.

6. Click the plus (+) or minus (-) sign next to the zoom so that the preview window resembles **Figure 6**.

There are six basic fractal shapes. You can choose each via the Fractal Map.

The six fractal shapes

1. Press on the Fractal Map to view the six fractal choices (**Figure 7**).
2. Choose each one of the choices listed.
3. At the magnification which was set in the previous steps, the Preview window for each of the shapes should look like **Figures 8–13**.

Figure 9. *The **Julia** shape.*

Figure 10. *The **M-J Hybrid I** shape.*

Figure 11. *The **M-J Hybrid II** shape.*

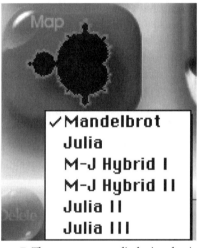

Figure 7. *The **pop-up menu** displaying the six fractal choices.*

Figure 12. *The **Julia II** shape.*

Figure 8. *The **Mandelbrot** shape.*

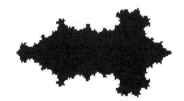

Figure 13. *The **Julia III** shape.*

Fractal shapes

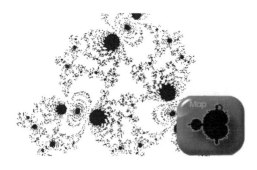

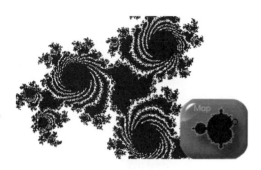

One of the fascinations of fractals is that they look different depending on where in the design you are looking and at what magnification. There are different techniques for moving around the shape.

Moving around a shape

1. Press on the Map panel to choose the Julia II fractal.

2. Hold the Command key and move the red circle in the map. The Preview window will change accordingly.

3. To position the design more precisely within the Preview window, press and drag within the Preview window.

4. Press on any of the arrows around the Preview window to also move the design within the Preview window.

5. Use **Figure 14** as a guide for moving around the Julia II fractal.

Tips

◆ The image shown on the Map panel is a Mandelbrot fractal. Therefore, if you are in the Mandelbrot fractal, moving the red circle to a point on the panel will show a similar view in the Preview window.

◆ The Mandelbrot fractal is the only design that is in the Map panel. Therefore, if you are in any of the other fractals, moving the red circle to a point on the panel will not show a similar view in the Preview window.

Figure 14. *Various previews of the **Julia II** shape and their corresponding maps.*

In addition to moving around a fractal, zooming in or out will also change the look of the design. There are several ways to zoom in or out of a design.

Zooming in and out of a design

1. Click on the plus (+) or minus (-) signs next to the Zoom Control to zoom in or out on a shape (**Figure 15**).

2. Position the magnifying glass cursor over the image and click to zoom in.

3. Hold the Option key and position the magnifying glass cursor over the image and click to zoom out.

Tip

◆ Some fractals reveal new details as you zoom in. Others are endless repeating patterns.

You can also use the Zoom slider to move quickly from one magnfication to another.

Using the Zoom slider

1. Press on the word Zoom to reveal the Zoom slider (**Figure 16**).

2. Drag the slider to the right to zoom in.

3. Drag the slider to the left to zoom out.

Tip

◆ The slider in the Zoom slider will always reset itself to 100% after a zoom.

Figure 15. *Click on the **Zoom plus** (+) or **minus** (-) **signs** to zoom in or out of an object.*

Figure 16. *The **Zoom slider** lets you zoom in greater amounts from one magnification to another.*

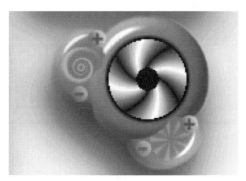

Figure 17. *The **Gradient Wrapping panel** controls how the colors of a gradient are displayed.*

Figure 18. *When the **Wrapping panel** is set to zero, only one color of the **Color Outside** gradient is visible around the fractal.*

In order to understand the effects of coloring a fractal design, you will need to clear the Gradient Wrapping panel.

Clearing the Gradient Wrapping panel

1. Click on the small spiral on the left side of the Wrapping panel (**Figure 17**). This will unwind the gradient so there is no spiral distortion applied to it.

2. Click on the small asterisk on the bottom right of the Wrapping panel. This will undo any repetitions of the gradient.

3. The large circle in the middle of the Wrapping panel will now be blank indicating no wrapping or repetitions have been applied.

The Fractal Explorer lets you apply colors and gradients to your design.

Changing the outside color

1. Press on the gradient ramp under the Color Outside to reveal the pop-up menu of preset gradients.

2. Under the category for Texture Blends, choose the first listing, a Full Intensity Hue Spectrum.

3. The full spectrum of color will appear in the ramp, however only the red will be seen in the fractal (**Figure 18**). This is because when the wrapping and repetition controls are blank, only one color from a gradient will be visible.

4. To see the effect of choosing other gradients, press on the Color Outside ramp and choose from the submenu.

The Loop setting controls the order of the gradient. This lets you choose which color of the gradient will be first.

Changing the Loop order

1. Make sure the gradient in the Color Outside ramp has a different color for the start and the end. (The Full Rainbow Spectrum, under Julia Set Gradients is a good choice.)

2. Press on the Loop control and choose Sawtooth: A to B (**Figure 19**). The outside color will be purple because purple is the first color of the gradient.

3. Press on the Loop control and choose Sawtooth: B to A. The outside color will be red because red is the last color.

Tips

◆ When the Wrapping Controls are blank, only the first and last colors of a gradient will be available using the loop controls.

◆ The two Triangular Loop choices do not have any effect on your design when the Wrapping Controls are blank.

You can also change the inside color of the fractal.

Changing the inside color

1. Press on the gradient ramp under the Color Inside.

2. Choose Solid White to change the inside color to white.

3. Choose Transparent to change the inside color to a transparent hole. The transparent setting is only evident if there is an image in the original file you are working on (**Figure 20**).

4. Choose the various other gradients to change the inside color.

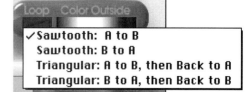

Figure 19. *The **Loop** menu controls the order of the gradient colors in the design.*

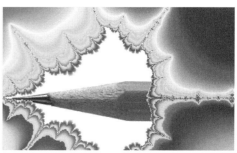

Figure 20. *Setting the interior color to* ***Transparent*** *allows you to see the image in the original file.*

Loop order; Inside color

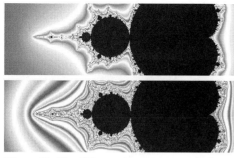

Figure 21. *The difference between **one spiral repetition** (top) and **three clicks to increase the spiral repetions** (bottom).*

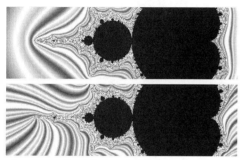

Figure 22. *The difference between **one repetition** (top) and **three repetitions** (bottom).*

Once you've chosen a gradient for the outside color, you can then use the Wrapping Controls to see the rest of that gradient's colors in the design.

Using the Wrapping Controls

1. Click on the plus (+) sign for the Spiral Control. Each click increases how often the colors of the gradients are repeated as they move from the center of the design (**Figure 21**).

2. Click on the plus (+) sign for the Repetition Control. Each click increases how often the colors of the gradient are repeated within each of the spiral reptitions (**Figure 22**).

Tips

◆ The minus (-) sign will decrease the winds of the spiral and the repetitions of the gradient.

◆ Clicking the minus (-) sign beyond the blank setting will change the order of the gradient repitition and the direction of the spiral. Further clicks will then increase the winds of the spiral and the repetitions of the gradient.

◆ The Color Inside will only show the first or last color of the gradient chosen. The Wrapping Controls do not affect the Color Inside gradient.

◆ The spiral is referred to as the Equipotential Speed in the Shuffle menu.

◆ The repetition is referred to as the Radial Speed in the Shuffle menu.

The Fractal Explorer also has an Opacity Control panel. This works much differently than the Opacity Control panel in the Kai's Power Tools 3.0 filters.

Using the Opacity Control panel

1. Press on the Opacity Control panel to display the opacity menu (**Figure 23**).

2. The Opacity menu lets you choose only what image will be displayed behind the preview window.

3. Choose Use Current Selection to have your design in front of the current image in the host application.

Tips

◆ Use the other settings in the Opacity Control panel to see what your design would look like if applied to other types of images. This can be helpful if you are creating presets for others to work with and you need to see how different designs would react with different images.

◆ None of the other settings in the Opacity Control panel will actually create the image you see in the Preview window. They are there solely for reference.

◆ The choice for Detail and Color displays a picture of Kai Krause, the "Kai" of Kai's Power Tools.

◆ While there is no range for opacity control in the Fractal Explorer, the Options menu lets you set the different apply modes. For a complete list of how the apply modes will affect your image and design, see Chapter 12, "Apply Modes."

Figure 23. *The **Opacity** menu lets you choose the type of image that will be displayed in the Preview window.*

All Parameters
None

✓**Exterior Colors**
✓**Interior Colors**
✓**Exterior Looping**
✓**Interior Looping**
  Apply Mode
  Test Image
✓**Equipotential Speed**
✓**Radial Speed**

Figure 24. *The Shuffle button menu lets you change the parameters that are changed by clicking on the Shuffle button.*

Once you have a design that you like, you may want to modify it slightly. You can do so with the Shuffle button.

Using the Shuffle button

1. Press and hold on the Shuffle button to display the Shuffle button menu (**Figure 24**).

2. Choose All Parameters to modify all the features of your fractal except the shape and zoom.

3. Choose None to turn off all the features and then add just the one or two that you want.

4. Once you have set the parameters of the Shuffle button, a plain click on the button will randomly change the features of your design.

Tips

◆ Turn off the Test Image if you want to continue to see your background image in the Preview window.

◆ Also, if you don't want the background image to show in the fractal, turn off the Apply Mode setting.

Shuffle button

Fractal designs often have details that are not visible at each magnification. The Detail Control lets you see those details as you zoom in on the design.

Using the Detail Control

1. To best understand the Detail Control, choose the Mandelbrot fractal.

2. Zoom in on the left side of the design. The design will show a certain amount of detail.

3. Press on the word Detail to reveal the Detail Control slider (**Figure 25**).

4. Move the slider all the way to the right to increase the amount of detail in the preview.

5. Zoom in on the left-most point of the Mandelbrot design. Changing the detail settings changes the shape of the design (**Figure 26**).

Tips

◆ The plus (+) sign control increases the amount of detail.

◆ The minus (-) sign control decreases the amount of detail.

Figure 25. *The **Detail Control** slider lets you change the amount of detail seen in the fractal shape.*

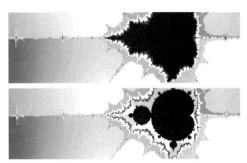

Figure 26. *The difference between **low detail setting** (top) and a **high detail setting** (bottom).*

Detail Control

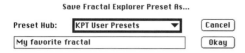

Figure 27. *The Save Fractal Explorer Preset dialog box lets you name and save your fractal settings.*

Once you've created a fractal design you like, you will want to store it for future work.

Storing fractal designs

1. Click on the Add button to bring up the Save Preset dialog box (**Figure 27**).

2. Give your fractal design a name and then click OK.

Once you have stored your design, you can then apply it using the Preset menu.

Using the Preset menu

1. Press on the triangle to display the presets that ship with the Fractal Explorer or the ones you have added.

2. Choose the preset and it will be applied to your preview.

Tip

◆ Some of the presets that ship with the Fractal Explorer, such as Santa Fe Glow, will change the Apply mode and the Opacity test image. This will change what you see in the Preview window.

APPLY MODES 12

All of the filters have different Apply modes which change how each of the effects will interact with the file from the host application. If you have a blank file, most of the Apply modes will not do anything. However, with files that contain images, each of the Apply modes will create different effects.

In this chapter you will learn:

◆ Where the Apply modes are located.

◆ The Normal Apply mode.

◆ The Procedural + Apply mode.

◆ The Procedural - Apply mode.

◆ The Darken Only Apply mode.

◆ The Light Only Apply mode.

◆ The Multiple Apply mode.

◆ The Screen Apply mode.

◆ The Difference Apply mode.

◆ The Add Apply mode.

◆ The Subtract Apply mode.

Locating the Apply modes

1. In the Spheroid Designer, Texture Explorer 2.1 and Fractal Explorer 2.1, the Apply modes are found under the Option menu.

2. In the Gradient Designer, the Texture Explorer, the Interform, and the Compact Filters, the Apply modes are found under the Glue Control panel.

3. In the Lens f/x filters, the Apply modes are found under the Glue Gauge.

Apply modes

Normal

In the Normal Apply mode, the effect is layered over the original file from the host application (**Figure 1**). For most effects this will create a totally opaque image. However, lowering the opacity, or using transparency colors, will allow portions of the original file to show through the effect.

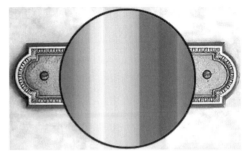

Figure 1. *The **Normal** Apply mode.*

Procedural +

In the Procedural + Apply mode, the effect is combined with the original file based on the luminance or brightness of the source image (**Figure 2**). This mode is excellent for wrapping a colored effect onto a grayscale image. In the 2.1 filters this was called Procedural Blend mode.

Procedural -

In the Procedural - Apply mode, the effect is combined with the original file based on the luminance or brightness of the effect colors (**Figure 3**). For most source images, this mode will allow more of the effect to be seen. In the 2.1 filters this was called the Reverse Blend mode.

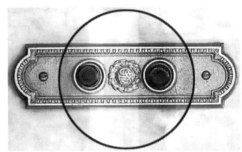

Figure 2. *The **Procedural** + Apply mode.*

Figure 3. *The **Procedural** - Apply mode.*

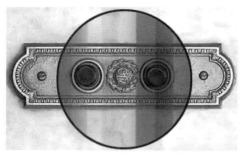

Figure 4. *The **Darken Only** Apply mode.*

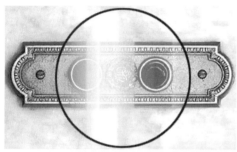

Figure 5. *The **Lighten Only** Apply mode.*

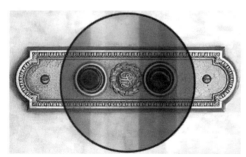

Figure 6. *The **Multiply** Apply mode.*

Darken Only

In the Darken Only Apply mode (**Figure 4**), the effect is applied only if the original image pixel is lighter than the color in the effect. If the original image pixel is darker than the color in the effect, then the original image is not changed. For most effects, this has the result of leaving blacks unchanged.

Lighten Only

In the Lighten Only Apply mode (**Figure 5**), the effect is applied only if the original image pixel is darker than the color in the effect. This is the exact opposite than the Darken Only mode.

Multiply

In the Multiply Apply mode (**Figure 6**), the effect and the original image are combined equally into one new image. This is similar to the effect of setting one image to overprint another in prepress instructions.

Screen

In the Screen Apply mode (**Figure 7**), the effect and the original image are combined in the exact opposite of the Multiply Apply mode. This is similar to the effect of bleaching out one image over another.

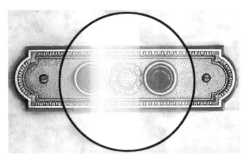

Figure 7. *The **Screen** Apply mode.*

Difference

In the Difference Apply mode (**Figure 8**), the effect and the original image are combined together to create an inversion, or negative image. The amount of the inversion depends on the color of the effect. Black areas of the effect will cause no change to the original image. White areas of the effect will be inverted completely. Any colors in between will be inverted according to how much darkness they have.

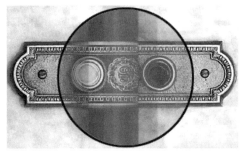

Figure 8. *The **Difference** Apply mode.*

Add

In the Add Apply mode (**Figure 9**), the effect and the original image are combined, adding their values together. This is similar to the effect of projecting two slides onto the same screen.

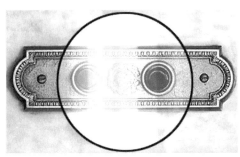

Figure 9. *The **Add** Apply mode.*

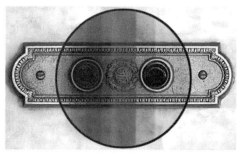

Figure 10. *The **Subtract** Apply mode.*

Subtract

In the Subtract Apply mode (**Figure 10**), the effect color is subtracted from the original image. This is similar to the effect of the Multiply Apply mode, but will change the colors of the effect.

Tip

◆ The Apply modes are work in a similar way to the layer and painting modes found in Adobe Photoshop.

CONVOLVER 13

S o far all the filters presented have been from Kai's Power Tools. Convolver is its own filter that is sold separately and works independently from KPT 3. There are two ways to use Convolver: as a serious production tool for color and image manipulation, or as a creative design tool. Whichever way you work with Convolver, you will need to work from within a host application.

In this chapter you will learn:

◆ Installing Convolver.

◆ The Convolver Interface elements.

◆ The Tweak Linear Convolution mode.

◆ The Tweak Unsharp/Gaussian mode.

◆ The Tweak Difference Mask mode.

◆ Using the Design mode.

◆ Using the Explore mode.

◆ Changing the views and preview modes.

◆ Storing settings using the Memory Dots and the Presets menu.

◆ Changing the Options and Preferences.

◆ Earning Stars.

Installing Convolver

1. Insert the Convolver disk and double click on the KPT Convolver.sea icon.

2. In the dialog box that appears, select the plug-ins folder of the host application that you want to use with Convolver. (See Chapter 2, "Installation" for more details and tips on installing filters in host applications.)

Convolver uses many of the Interface elements from KPT 3.0. Watch out, though, there are new elements and others that work differently.

INTERFACE

There are three different modes for Convolver which means you can't see all of the controls at one time (**Figure 1**). Depending on which mode you are working in, some of the controls will be dimmed out.

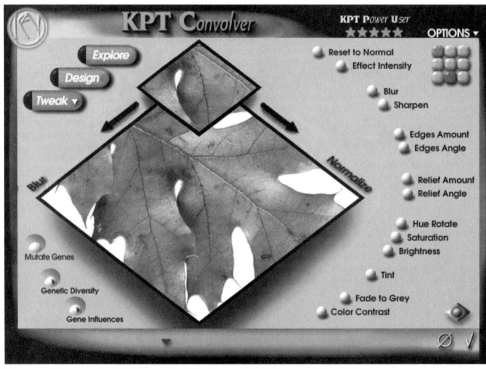

Figure 1. *The complete **KPT Convolver** interface with **all the controls visible**.*

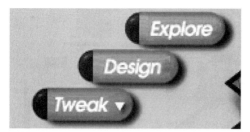

Figure 2. *The three buttons for the **Tweak**, **Design**, and **Explore** modes.*

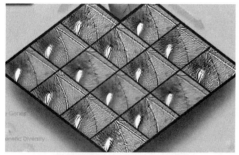

Figure 3. *The **Grid/Preview Diamond** in the **Grid mode** (top) and in the **Preview mode** (bottom).*

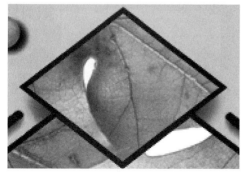

Figure 4. *The **Current Tile** diamond.*

Mode buttons

Click on each of the mode buttons (**Figure 2**) to switch from one mode to another.

Tip

◆ Another way to switch modes is to click on any dimmed-out control, That will activate the mode that the control is used for.

Grid/Preview Diamond

The Grid/Preview Diamond (**Figure 3**) has two different looks. In the Grid mode, it shows the variations and changes that will be applied to the image. In the Preview mode, it shows a large-size preview of the image being changed.

Current Tile

The Current Tile (**Figure 4**) is the diamond at the top of the Grid/Preview Diamond. It serves two purposes. When the Grid/Preview Diamond is in the Grid mode, the Current Tile serves as the Preview of how the effect is currently being applied to the image. The Current Tile also serves as a toggle button. Click in the Current Tile to switch between the Grid/Preview modes.

Explore controls

The Explore mode has three sunken marble controls (**Figure 5**). These control the variations applied to the image.

Axis arrows

The Axis arrows (**Figure 6**) are seen in the Design mode. They indicate the direction of the effect within the Grid/Preview Diamond. They can also be manipulated to increase or decrease an effect.

Effect names

The Effect names (**Figure 7**) are seen in the Design mode. They act as both a pop-up menu to show all the effects available and a toggle to switch from one effect to its reverse.

Effect menu

The Effect menu (**Figure 8**) is seen in the Design mode. Press on the Effect name to display the Effect menu. Choose which effect you want to use.

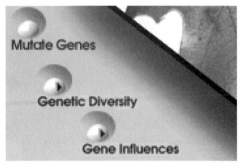

Figure 5. *The **Mutate Genes**, **Genetic Diversity**, and **Gene Influences** controls.*

Figure 6. *The **Axis arrows**.*

Figure 7. *The **Effect names**.*

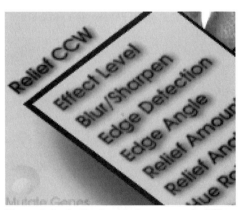

Figure 8. *In the **Design mode**, press on the **Effect name** to see the **Effect menu**.*

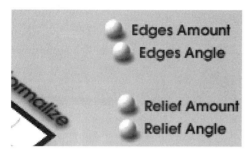

Figure 9. *The Effect marbles.*

Figure 10. *The **Tweak** mode choices. **Linear Convolution** is the basic mode for working with Convolver. **Unsharp/Gaussian** and **Difference Mask** are used for special effects.*

Effect marbles

The Effect marbles (**Figure 9**) are seen in the Tweak mode. Pressing on a marble and dragging to the right will increase the effect. Pressing on the marble and dragging to to left will decrease the effect.

Tip

◆ Working with the marbles is tricky. They act much like slider controls, but as soon as you start the drag, your mouse cursor will disappear. Keep pressing and dragging. The Info Area at the bottom of the Convolver screen will give you a read-out of the effect.

The best way to understand Convolver is to start with a file with some sort of image in it. Do not use a blank file.

Opening Convolver

1. Open a file in the host application.
2. Choose KPT Convolver 1.0 from the KPT Convolver menu.
3. You will now work inside Convolver. You will not go back to the host application until you are done.

TWEAK LINEAR CONVOLUTION MODE

The default settings of Convolver depend on how the program was last used. In order to better understand the features, you will need to clear the settings and switch to the Tweak mode.

Clearing the Tweak mode settings

1. Press on the Tweak mode control and choose Linear Convolution from the pop-up menu (**Figure 10**).
2. Click the Reset to Normal marble to start with blank settings.

Most of the Convolver settings are paired features. A positive amount of one setting is actually the negative amount of the other. Where appropriate, each of the pairs will be presented together.

Tips

◆ As you drag, the amount you are changing the effect will appear in the blank area at the bottom of the Convolver area.

◆ Double click directly on the marble to reset the effect to 0%.

Using Blur/Sharpen

1. Press on the Blur marble and drag to the right. This will add a blur to your image (**Figure 11**).

2. Press on the Sharpen marble and drag to the right. This will sharpen your image (**Figure 12**).

3. Drag to the left on the Blur marble to sharpen the image. Drag to the left on the Sharpen marble to blur the image.

Using Edges Amount/Edges Angle

1. Press on the Edges Amount marble and drag to the right to apply the effect. The Edges effect applies a type of directional sharpening (**Figure 13a**).

2. Press on the Edges Angle marble (**Figure 13b**) and drag in either direction to change the angle of the Edges effect.

Tip

◆ If no Edges amount is applied, then changing the Edges angle will have no effect on the image.

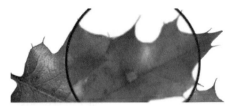

Figure 11. *The **Blur** effect.*

Figure 12. *The **Sharpen** effect.*

Figure 13a. *The **Edges Amount** effect.*

Figure 13b. *The same **Edges Amount** effect applied with a different **Edges Angle**.*

Blur/Sharpen; Edges Amount/Edge Angle

Figure 14a. *The **Relief Amount** effect.*

Figure 14b. *The same **Relief Amount** effect applied with a different **Relief Angle**.*

Figure 15. *The **Hue Rotate** effect.*

Figure 16. *The **Saturation** effect set to increase the saturation of the colors.*

Figure 17. *The **Brightness** effect set to increase the brightness of the image.*

Using Relief Amount/Relief Angle

1. Press on the Relief Amount marble and drag to the right to apply the effect. The Relief effect applies an embossing effect without losing color information (**Figure 14a**).

2. Press on the Relief Angle marble (**Figure 14b**) and drag in either direction to change the angle of the Relief effect.

Using Hue Rotate

Drag to the left or right on the Hue Rotate marble to change all the colors in your image (**Figure 15**).

Using Saturation

Drag to the left or right on the Saturation marble to decrease or increase the saturation in your image (**Figure 16**).

Using Brightness

Drag to the left or right on the Brightness marble to decrease or increase the brightness in your image (**Figure 17**).

Using Tint

Press on the Tint marble (**Figure 18**) to
see the tint color wheel and choose a color
to tint your image (**Figure 19**).

Tip

◆ The Tint marble is not available when
you first open Convolver. It is available
by earning Convolver Stars. See the
section later in this chapter on how to
earn the Stars.

Using Fade to Grey

Drag to the right to gradually fade all
color values to grey. Dragging to the left
restores those values.

Using Color Contrast

Drag to the left or right on the Color
Control marble to decrease or increase the
contrast among colors in your image.

Reset to Normal

Click on the Reset to Normal marble
(**Figure 20**) to change the settings for all
the marbles back to zero.

Effect Intensity

Drag on the Effect Intensity marble
(**Figure 20**) to adjust all the effects
together. For instance, if the blur is 20%,
the brightness is 50%, and relief amount
is 70%, when you drag on the Effect
Intensity marble, all three effects change
will together, maintaining the relationship
between their settings.

TWEAK UNSHARP/GAUSSIAN MODE

Press on the Tweak mode control to
choose the Unsharp/Gaussian mode. This
mode changes the Blur and Sharpen
marbles to the Gaussian and Unsharp
(**Figure 21**). It adds the Radius and
Threshold marbles and eliminates the
Edges and Relief marbles.

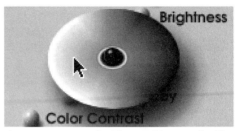

Figure 18. *Press on the* **Tint** *marble to see the* **Tint**
Color Wheel.

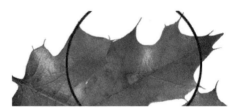

Figure 19. *The* **Tint** *effect.*

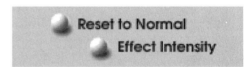

Figure 20. *Click on the* **Reset to Normal** *marble*
to reset all the effects and drag on the **Effect**
Intensity *to increase or decrease the effects.*

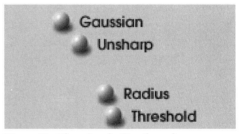

Figure 21. *Changing the Tweak mode to*
Gaussian/Unsharp *displays the* **Gaussian**,
Unsharp, **Radius**, *and* **Threshold** *marbles.*

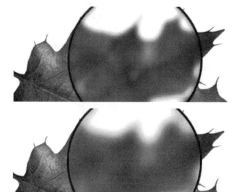

Figure 22. *Top: the **Gaussian** blur applied with a low **Radius** setting. Bottom: the same **Gaussian** blur with a high **Radius**.*

Figure 23. *The **Unsharp Mask** filter set to high, with a low **Radius** and low **Threshold**.*

Figure 24. *The **Unsharp Mask** filter set to high, with a high **Radius** and low **Threshold**.*

Figure 25. *The **Unsharp Mask** filter set to high, with a high **Radius** and high **Threshold**.*

Using Gaussian and Radius

Drag to the left or right on the Gaussian marble to decrease or increase the Gaussian Blur applied to your image.

Drag to the left or right on the Radius marble to add to the intensity of the Gaussian blur. This means that at a low radius, a certain Gaussian blur amount will look different than the same blur amount at a high radius (**Figure 22**).

Using Unsharp, Radius and Threshold

Drag to the left or right on the Unsharp marble to decrease or increase the Unsharp masking applied to your image (**Figure 23**). (Unsharp masking, despite the name, is actually a sharpening technique. Unlike ordinary sharpening, at high settings Unsharp mask does not pixelate the image.)

Drag to the left or right on the Radius marble to decrease or increase the unsharp masking applied to your image (**Figure 24**). This is similar to how the radius marble works on the Gaussian blur.

Drag to the left or right on the Threshold marble to decrease or increase the Unsharp masking applied to your image. Increasing the Threshold will have the result of lowering the amount of Unsharp masking applied to the image (**Figure 25**).

TWEAK DIFFERENCE MASK MODE

Press on the Tweak mode control to choose the Difference Mask mode. This mode will apply a difference effect between the original image and the current effect settings.

In the Difference Mask mode, drag to the left or right on any of the marbles. The effects will be applied through the Difference Mask (**Figure 26**).

Tip

◆ Because the Difference Mask relies on the difference between the original image and the effect being applied, the image will be black if all the effects are at the Normal setting.

Once you've worked in the Tweak mode, you should understand the different Convolver effects. You can then switch to the Design mode which gives you a way of anticipating how the effects will look when applied to your image.

DESIGN MODE

1. Click on the Design mode control at the top of the Convolver screen.

2. Press on one of the Effect Names to see the Effect menu. Choose the effect you want.

3. Each of the grid choices applies the effect in increasing amounts. The further away from the top the more the effect will be applied (**Figure 27**).

4. Drag the Axis Arrows (**Figure 28**) to change the amount of the effect being applied across the grid.

5. Click on one of the grid choices to apply it to the original image. The grid will then reflect how the effects would then be reapplied to the image.

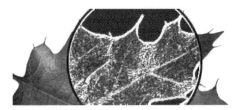

Figure 26. *The **Difference Mask** effect.*

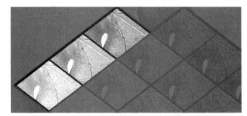
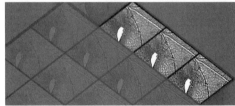

Figure 27. *The **grid squares** that control mixture of the effects. Top: only the **left effect** applied. Bottom: only the **right effect** applied. Middle: **both effects** applied equally.*

Figure 28. *Pressing and dragging on the **Axis Arrows** changes the amount of the effect.*

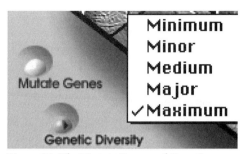

Figure 29. *The Mutate Genes and Genetic Diversity controls of the Explore mode.*

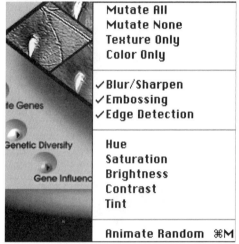

Figure 30. *The Gene Influences menu of the Explore mode.*

The last mode is the Explore mode. Instead of adjusting every single effect in a different way, the Explore mode lets you apply the effects with random variations. This is similar to the Mutation Trees in Kai's Power Tools.

EXPLORE MODE

1. Click on the Explore mode control at the top of the Convolver screen.

2. Press on the Genetic Diversity sunken marble (**Figure 29**) to see the pop-up menu. This controls how much mutation is applied in the Explore mode.

3. Press on the Gene Influences sunken marble (**Figure 30**) to see the pop-up menu. This controls which effects will be changed during the mutation.

4. Click on the Mutate Genes sunken marble to apply the mutation.

5. Click as needed until you see a preview in the Grid that you like.

6. Click on the preview in the Grid that you like. The original image will change to reflect that mutation. The Grid will then change with a new set of mutations.

Tips

◆ The Texture Only command means that only Blur/Sharpen, Embossing, and Edge Detection will be mutated.

◆ The Color Only command means that only Hue, Saturation, Brightness, Contrast, and Tint will be mutated.

Explore mode

The Split Screen Preview allows you to compare the current effect settings to the original image.

Split Screen Preview

1. In the Design or Explore modes, click on the Current Tile to replace the Grid Diamond with the Preview window. (The Tweak mode is always in the Preview window.)

2. Click on the Split Screen Preview button (**Figure 31**) at the lower right corner of the Convolver screen.

3. The left side will of the Preview window will show the original image. The right side of the Preview window will show the image with the current effect applied (**Figure 32**).

Tip

◆ The Split Screen Preview is made available by earning Stars. See the section later in this chapter on how to earn the Stars.

You may find that with certain images, especially large ones, the area you want to see lies outside the diamond window area. You then need to change the View area within the diamond.

Change View area

1. Hold the Control key and then press and drag around the Preview window. This will give you a diamond shaped cursor that can be positioned over the area you want to see in the Preview window (**Figure 33**).

2. Release the mouse to go back to the main screen.

Figure 31. *The Split Screen Preview control.*

Figure 32. *Viewing in the Split Screen Preview.*

Figure 33. *Holding the Control key and dragging lets you change the View area.*

Figure 34. *The Memory Dots grid.*

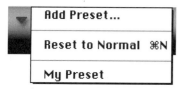

Figure 35. *The Preset Triangle and Preset menu.*

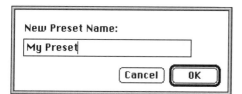

Figure 36. *The Preset dialog box.*

Once you have an effect that you like, you can save it to apply to other images. You can do so with Memory Dots or Presets.

Using Memory Dots

1. Click on one of the gray Memory Dots (**Figure 34**). The dot will turn dark brown indicating that the settings have been temporarily stored in Convolver.

2. To load a Memory Dot, click on it. The dot will turn red indicating that it has been applied.

3. To clear a Memory Dot, Option-click on it. The dot will turn gray.

4. To save the nine Memory Dot settings, choose Command-S or Save Dots from the Options menu.

5. To load the settings of saved dots, choose Command-L or Load Dots from the Options menu.

Tip

◆ The Memory Dots panel is made available by earning Stars. See the section later in this chapter on how to earn the Stars.

Presets let you store settings with descriptive names.

Presets menu

1. Press on the Presets triangle at the bottom of the Convolver screen. The Presets menu will appear (**Figure 35**).

2. To store a preset, choose Add Preset. The Preset dialog box (**Figure 36**) will appear.

3. Give your preset a name.

4. To load a preset, press on the Presets triangle and choose the preset from the bottom of the menu.

Memory Dots; Presets menus

The Options menu (**Figure 37**) contains choices about Convolver operations as well as lets you choose the Preferences dialog box (**Figure 38**).

Options

1. Choose Kernel Matrices to see a numerical read-out of how your choices are changing your image.

2. Choosing Comparison Grid Overlay puts a grid frame over the entire preview image and then shows the mutations within each tile.

3. Choosing Reselect Sample performs the same function as the Control-Drag command.

4. Choose Current Selection to use the current image in the Preview window.

5. Choose Color - Cool Car, Edges/Relief - Hand Lines, or Creative Multi Effects - Eye to put a sample image in the Preview window.

Convolver Preferences

1. Choose Return to Previous state to have Convolver open at the same settings that were in effect the last time it was used.

2. Choose Monochrome Design menus to change the menus in the design mode to ordinary vertical, black and white, Chicago font menus. (This is helpful on slower machines.)

3. Choose Virtual Mouse to help use the marble sliders in the Tweak mode.

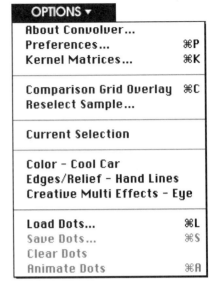

Figure 37. *The Options menu.*

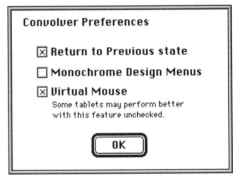

Figure 38. *The Convolver Preferences choices.*

Congratulations !

You have attained your first Star, indicating you have passed through each Convolver mode at least once.

As you continue to work with KPT Convolver, you will earn more stars along the way. With each new Star, you will be awarded a new tool to further enhance your Convolver "tool-belt." Stars are awarded according to your need, based on frequency of specific functions used. They will not necessarily appear in any particular order...

We hope you enjoy this unfolding functionality... keep an eye on the stars, and when you get to five stars, feel free to gloat!

★ teamCONVO

Figure 39. *The Stars award.*

Among the debated features of Convolver are the Stars that you "earn" as you work in the program. (Some people love 'em; others hate 'em.) As you earn each Star, you are given more features to work with. If you want, you can earn your Stars by working with the program, or you can cheat to get them all at once.

Earning Stars

1. Click on each mode (Explore, Tweak, and Design) and adjust something in each mode. This gives you the first Star which adds no feature (**Figure 39**).

2. In the Explore or Design mode, click repeatedly on the Current Tile diamond. This gives you the second Star which adds the split screen control.

3. In the Tweak mode, press and drag on the Tint marble for a while. This gives you the third Star which add the Tint Color Wheel.

4. Switch repeatedly between the three modes. This gives the fourth Star which adds the Memory Dots.

5. In the Explore or Design mode, drag on any of the grid sections and drag your mouse in a circle over any one of the grid sections. This is called Scrubbing. Scrubbing adjusts effects without using arrows or mutations. This gives you the fifth Star which adds animation to the changes.

Tip

◆ You can cheat to get your Stars by pressing the Command-Option-Control-Shift keys, double-clicking on the Mutate Genes sunken marble, and then clicking on the Kai Logo. However, Stars you get by cheating are temporary and disappear when you quit the host application.

METAPHOTOS 14

Thir chapter covers working with the more than 2200 different stock photos available from MetaTools. Originally sold as PowerPhotos, they are now available as MetaPhotos. MetaPhotos are available on CD-ROM, or they can be purchased via the MetaTools web site. In fact, all of the photographic images in this book are from MetaPhotos collections.

So why a chapter on collections of photos? Because it is not enough to just open a photo. You want to be able to make composite images like the illustration on the opposite page. To so so you need to work with the alpha channels and paths in the images.

All of the exercises in this chapter assume you are working with Adobe Photoshop 4. If you have another program, consult its manual for the equivalent techniques.

In this chapter you will learn

◆ The difference between HiRes and LoRes formats.

◆ How to change the resolution and dimensions of HiRes images.

◆ Using the built-in Alpha Channels to create composite images, drop shadows and glows.

◆ Using the Transflectance Channels to make more realistic composites.

◆ How to create paths from the built-in Alpha Channels.

◆ How to create EPS files with Clipping Paths.

Choosing HiRes or LoRes files

MetaPhotos come in two different resolutions: HiRes and LoRes. If you are working on web designs or a layout to show a client, you probably can use just the LoRes versions of the images. This means your file will take up far less space on your hard disk, and will be much faster to work with. If you are doing work for final print output, you will most likely need the HiRes versions.

Once you have chosen a HiRes file, you should check to see if it is the right size for final output. To do that, you will need to change the image size.

Changing HiRes file sizes

1. With a HiRes image open, choose Image Size from the Image menu. The Image Size dialog box will appear (**Figure 1**).

2. Make sure that the Resample Image checkbox is selected.

3. To change the size of the file using the physical dimensions, highlight the amount in either the Width or Height fields.

4. Enter the new amount.

5. If you want to change the amount by a specific percentage, or to a different unit of measurement, press on the pop-up menu to the right of the fields (**Figure 2**).

6. Click OK to change the file.

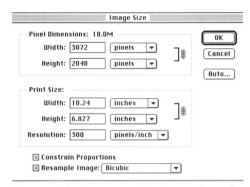

Figure 1. *The Image Size dialog box can be used to change the physical dimensions or resolution of an image.*

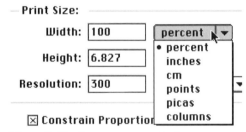

Figure 2. *Use the pop-up menu to change a dimension by percentage or a different unit of measurement.*

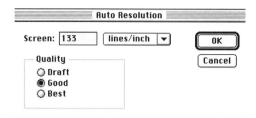

Figure 3. *The Auto Resolution dialog box allows you to set the resolution based on the final output linescreen.*

Tips

◆ Watch the Pixel Dimensions area of the Image Size box. It will show you the old file size and what the new one will be.

◆ Once you have changed a measurement using percentage or a different unit of measurement, you can use the pop-up menu to go back to inches or some other unit.

◆ Hold the Option key to turn the Cancel button into a Reset button. This allows you to change all the fields back to their original values and then start again.

◆ Click on the Auto button to use the Auto Resolution dialog box (**Figure 3**). This allows you to set the resolution based on the line screen at which the image will be printed and the desired image quality.

Alpha Channels

Alpha Channels is the technical term for special channels of information that can be stored with images. Many of the MetaPhotos contain Alpha Channels for those images the you would like to select as silhouettes. These are typically still life images and poses of people. The images of landscapes, backgrounds, and textures do not typically contain Alpha Channels.

One of the most common uses for Alpha Channels is to select a single object within an image. The selected image can then be copied or dragged into other images.

Using Alpha Channels to create composite images

1. Open the image and then choose Show Channels from the Window menu.

2. If the image has an Alpha Channel it will appear as a numbered channel (**Figure 4**).

3. Drag the numbered Alpha Channel onto the Load channel selection icon or hold the Command key and click on the Alpha Channel.

4. The contours of the Alpha Channel will be the outline of the selection around the image (**Figure 5**).

5. Use the Move tool to drag the image from one picture to another.

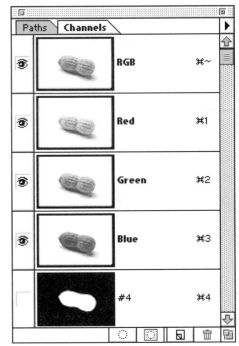

Figure 4. *The **Alpha Channel** is the numbered channel in the **Channels** palette.*

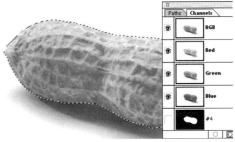

Figure 5. *The **Alpha Channel** contours are the outline formed for the selection.*

Figure 6. *The outlines of a selection can be dragged to offset a drop shadow.*

Figure 7. *Holding the **Command** and **Option** keys will subtract an **Alpha Channel** from the current selection.*

Figure 8. *A **fuzzy drop shadow** created without any layers.*

One of the most popular effects is to create a fuzzy drop shadow behind an image. If you are working with layers, it is relatively easy to use multiple layers to create the effect. However, you can also use Alpha Channels to create this effect without having to add layers to your image.

Using Alpha Channels to create a drop shadow:

1. Drag the numbered Alpha Channel onto the Load channel selection icon or hold the Command key and click on the Alpha Channel.

2. The contours of the Alpha Channel will be the outline of the selection around the image.

3. Use the Marquee tool to drag the outline away from the original image to the position where you want the shadow to be placed (**Figure 6**).

4. Apply the Feather command in whatever softness amount you want for your shadow.

5. Hold the Command and Option keys and click on the Alpha Channel (**Figure 7**). This will subtract the original Alpha Channel selection from the area now selected.

6. Adjust the Input and Output sliders in the Levels command to darken the selected area (**Figure 8**).

Creating drop shadows

A similar technique to creating a fuzzy drop shadow is to create a glow around an object. Again, while many people use layers to create this effect, you can accomplish the same look rather easily with an Alpha Channel.

Using Alpha Channels to create a glow

1. Use the Lasso tool set to a feathered amount to draw an irregular outline around the object you want to glow (**Figure 9**).

2. Hold the Command and Option keys and click on the Alpha Channel to subtract the original channel selection from the area selected.

3. Fill with a color or use the Input and Output sliders in the Levels command to create the glow (**Figure 10**).

Figure 9. *Creating an irregular selection with the* **Lasso** *tool.*

Figure 10. *The irregular selection can then be turned into a glow.*

Creating a glow

Figure 11. *The need for a **Transflectance Channel** is shown here as these glasses and bottle do not let the background image show through.*

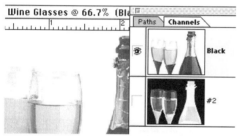

Figure 12. *A **Transflectance Channel** is a negative grayscale version of the image.*

Figure 13. *Using a **Transflectance Channel**, the wine glasses and bottle are pasted onto the image allowing the background image to show through.*

If you are working with an image such as a wine glass, or bottle, or any other image that is transparent, you may find that when you cut and paste the image from one background it doesn't look right in the new background (**Figure 11**).

This is why some of the images in the MetaPhotos collections have what is called Transflectance Channels. These are special types of Alpha Channel images that can be used to make selections that are more realistic when pasted from one illustration into another.

Using Transflectance Channels

1. To determine if an Alpha Channel contains a Transflectance Channel, click on the Alpha Channel in the Channels palette.

2. If the image in the Alpha Channel is a plain silhouette with no details of the items, it is an ordinary Alpha Channel.

3. If the image in the Alpha Channel is a grayscale negative version of the original, then it is a Transflectance Channel (**Figure 12**).

4. With the regular image visible, hold the Command key and click on the Transflectance Channel.

5. Copy or drag the selection from one image to another. Because you used a Transflectance Channel to select the image, you will be able to see through the pasted object to the original background (**Figure 13**).

Transflectance Channels

If an image contains an Alpha Channel, it most likely will also contain a path. This is a vector object that can be used to create a proper silhouette for use in programs such as QuarkXPress and Adobe PageMaker. You need to designate the path as a Clipping path. Without a Clipping path, it is not possible to layer one picture over another object and get a clean silhouette (**Figure 14**).

Figure 14. *A demonstration of the type of problem that can happen when a picture is layered over a background color without using the* **Clipping path**. *Notice the white areas filling in around the lamp.*

Creating a path

1. Open the Path palette. If there is no path listed, you can create one from the Alpha Channel.

2. In the Channels palette, hold the Command key and click on the Alpha Channel to create a selection.

3. In the Paths palette, choose Make Work path from the submenu or click on the icon (**Figure 15**). The Work path will appear.

4. Double click on the Work path to see the Save Path dialog box (**Figure 16**).

5. Once you have named your path, it will appear in the Paths palette.

Creating a Clipping path

1. Choose Clipping path from the Path submenu. The Clipping path dialog box (**Figure 17**) will appear.

2. Use the pop-up menu to choose the path as the Clipping path.

3. Save your file in the EPS (for QuarkXPress) or the TIFF (for PageMaker) formats.

Tip

◆ Clipping path names in Photoshop are written in the Paths palette in outline type. Regular path names are written in ordinary type.

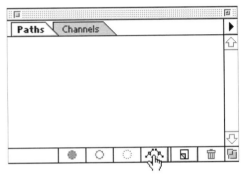

Figure 15. *Click on the* Make Work path *icon to turn a selection into a path.*

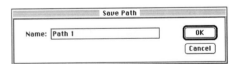

Figure 16. *After you create a* **Work path**, *you need to save it with a name.*

Figure 17. *Once you have a path, you can then designate it as a* **Clipping Path**.

KPT ACTIONS 15

I f you are running Kai's Power Tools 3 through the host application Adobe Photoshop 4, you have another tool available—KPT Actions.

KPT Actions is an accessory kit that adds the ability to script the settings of Kai's Power Tools filters. In addition, KPT Actions provides a collection of a hundred presets that create instant backgrounds, textures, frames, buttons, and effects.

In this chapter you will learn

◆ Requirements for running KPT Actions.

◆ Installing KPT Actions.

◆ Adding KPT Actions presets.

◆ Running actions in Photoshop.

◆ Running Text Effects actions.

◆ Running Frame actions.

◆ Running Buttons and Backgrounds actions.

◆ Recording a simple action.

◆ Modifying an existing action.

Requirements

The KPT Actions Installer requires Kai's Power Tools 3 and Photoshop 4. If you are running Kai's Power Tools through an earlier version of Photoshop, or another host application, you can't use KPT Actions. The KPT Actions Installer adds scripting (actions) capability to Kai's Power Tools 3. You will then be able to add the KPT filters to the Photoshop Actions Palette.

Installing KPT Actions

1. Locate the KPT Actions Installer icon on the KPT Actions CD-ROM.

2. Double-click on the KPT Actions Installer (**Figure 1**) icon to begin installation.

3. The installation dialog box first displays a Read Me file containing important information. Click the Continue button after you finish reading the Read Me file.

4. Once the Installer finds the folder containing Kai's Power Tools for Photoshop 4, click Update.

5. When the Intaller is finished, you will need to restart your computer.

6. You can then open Photoshop in the usual manner.

Once you have run the Installer to update your copy of Kai's Power Tools, you will also want to add the KPT Actions presets to the Photoshop Actions palette.

Adding the KPT Actions presets

1. Launch Photoshop 4. If the Photoshop Actions palette is not open, choose Window>Show Actions.

2. Press on the triangle in the upper right corner of the Actions palette and choose Load Actions.

3. Locate the KPT Actions folder on the KPT Actions CD-ROM and load the KPT Actions (**Figure 2**). This loads all the categories of actions at once.

4. If you have only a minimal amount of RAM allocated to Photoshop, you should load only the individual sets of Actions.

KPT Actions™ Installer

Figure 1. *Running the **KPT Actions Installer** allows you to update your copy of Kai's Power Tools so that they have scripting capability.*

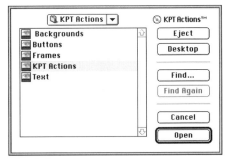

Figure 2. *Use the **Load Actions** command to find and load the complete set of actions.*

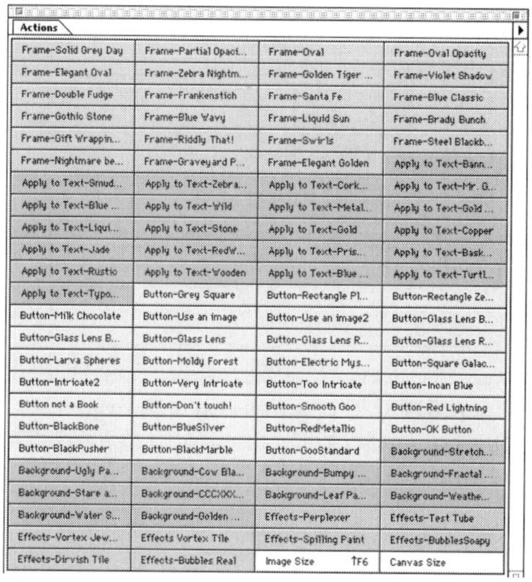

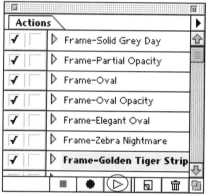

Figure 3. *Clicking on any of the buttons when the **Actions** palette is in the **Button mode** will place the action.*

Once you have installed KPT Actions, you will see one hundred actions presets added to your Photoshop Actions palette.

Running Actions in Photoshop

1. In the Button mode, the KPT Actions appear as single colored buttons (**Figure 3**) which can be played by clicking once on any action.

2. To play the actions when Button mode is not active, click once on the Action you would like to play and then press the VCR-like play button located at the bottom of the Actions palette (**Figure 4**).

Actions

		Frame-Solid Grey Day
✓	▷	Frame-Partial Opacity
✓	▷	Frame-Oval
✓	▷	Frame-Oval Opacity
✓	▷	Frame-Elegant Oval
✓	▷	Frame-Zebra Nightmare
✓	▷	**Frame-Golden Tiger Strip**

Figure 4. *Clicking the **Play button** (circled) at the bottom of the **Actions** palette will run an action.*

There are five categories of KPT Actions: Frames, Text, Buttons, Effects and Backgrounds. Some of the actions require specific types of images.

Running Text actions

1. The top layer should contain text on a transparent layer.

2. The bottom layer should contain a white background.

3. The text layer should be selected (**Figure 5**).

Running Frame actions

1. Open the single-layer image open that you would like to frame.

2. Choose the Frame action you would like to frame the image.

Tips

◆ Frame actions leave your original image on a separate layer from the frame. This allows you to color or otherwise modify the frame that is created.

◆ Frame actions add to the size of your final image (**Figure 6**).

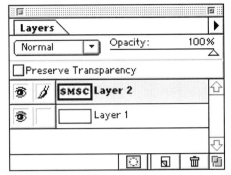

Figure 5. *The **Text actions** require two layers. The text should be on a transparent top layer which is selected.*

Figure 6. *The original image (top) and the same image (bottom) after running a **Frame action**. Notice the size of the image has enlarged to hold the frame.*

Figure 7. *Certain actions such as **Effects-Soapy Bubbles** require an image for the effect to work.*

Running Buttons and Backgrounds actions

1. The Buttons and Backgrounds actions can be run just by pressing the Action button or the Play icon.

2. The Buttons and Backgrounds actions will create a new image with the effect applied to it.

3. None of the Buttons or Backgrounds actions require that an image be open with the exception of Effects-Bubbles Real, Effects-Bubbles Soapy, Button-Use an Image and Button-Use an Image 2 (**Figure 7**).

Tip

◆ While those effects require an image, that image can still be a blank or plain colored file.

While KPT Actions presets are extremely powerful, and allow you to create amazing artwork, you can also use the scripting ability to create your own effects. If you have been working with Photoshop 4, you already know how easy it is to record actions. With KPT Actions, you can now add Kai's Power Tools filters into your recorded actions. In the following exercise you will record your steps to create a simple action. In this case you will create a "dirty" button that can be used for multimedia or Internet pages (**Figure 8**).

Recording a simple action

1. Click on the New Action button at the bottom of the Actions palette (**Figure 9**). Name the action Dirty Button and then click Record.

2. Choose New from the File menu and set the new document as Width: 200 pixels, Height: 200 pixels, Resolution: 72, Mode: RGB, Contents: White. Then click OK.

3. Click on the Default foreground colors button to restore the colors and then click on the Switch foreground colors to reverse them.

4. Choose Clouds from the Render submenu of the Filter menu and then choose Difference Clouds from the same Render submenu.

5. Choose Levels from the Adjust submenu of the Image menu. Move the white input slider so that its amount is at 100 and then move the gray input slider so that its amount is at 1.00. Click OK.

Figure 8. *Recording a set of commands will create a **Dirty Button** for use in multimedia or Internet pages.*

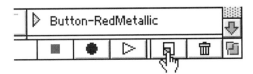

Figure 9. *Click the **New Action** button to start recording a new action.*

Figure 10. *The **Stop Recording** button stops the recording of the action.*

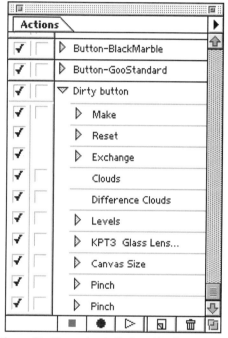

Figure 11. *The **action** is displayed in the **Actions Palette**.*

6. Choose KPT Glass Lens with the Mode: Normal, Glue: Normal, and Opacity: 100%. Click the green OK button.

7. Choose Image Size from the Image menu and change the width and height amounts to 120%. Click OK.

8. Choose Pinch from the Distort submenu of the Filter menu. Set the amount to -100. Click OK. Do this step again.

9. Choose Stop Recording (**Figure 10**) from the Actions submenu. The complete action (**Figure 11**) is now ready for playing.

Tips

◆ Don't rush! There is no time limit for recording actions.

◆ You will be creating a file as you work so you can judge your results.

◆ If you choose an incorrect command, just keep going. You can drag unneeded actions into the Actions panlette trash can after you have finished recording.

◆ Keep the Actions palette visible as you work so you can see each new command added to the action you are recording.

Recording a simple action

You don't have to be an expert to get the most out of KPT Actions. You can also modify the intricate actions that ship with KPT Actions to create your own looks. For this exercise you will take a simple action and change one of the KPT filters used in that action.

Figure 12. *Drag an action down to the New Action icon to duplicate that action.*

Modifying an existing action

1. Find the action Effects-Perplexer in the Actions palette and then drag the action to the New aciton icon (**Figure 12**) at the bottom of the palette. This creates a duplicate action named Effects-Perplexer Copy. You will work on this copy rather than the original action.

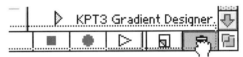

Figure 13. *Drag an action down to the Delete Action icon to delete that action.*

2. Click on the small triangle next to the Effects-Perplexer Copy to open the action.

3. Drag the second of the three KPT3 Gradient Designer commands onto the Delete Action icon (**Figure 13**). This deletes that command.

4. Drag the command KPT3 Texture Explorer onto the New Action icon. This creates a copy of that command.

5. Double click on the copy of the KPT3 Texture Explorer command you just created. This opens the Texture Explorer and allows you to record new settings for that command.

Modifying an existing action

Figure 14. *The difference between the **original Effects-Perplexer action** (top) and the **modified version of that action** (bottom).*

6. Hold the Spacebar as you press on the white triangle at the bottom of the Texture Explorer and then choose Bosch 1999 from the Presets list.

7. Press on the Glue panel and choose Procedural -.

8. Press on the Opacity Control Panel and lower the opacity to 70%.

9. Click the OK button to return to Photoshop. Press the Play button to see how the Effects-Perplexer Copy differs from the original (**Figure 14**).

Modifying an existing action

INDEX

3D Stereo Noise filter, 97
    illustrated, 26
    opening, 97
    using, 97
    See also Compact Filters

A

Acrobat Reader, 11
Add Apply mode, 134
Add Preset button, 29, 38, 78, 115
alias folder, 9
Alpha Channels, 156-159
    composite image creation with, 156
    contours, 156
    defined, 156
    drop shadow creation with, 157
    glow creation with, 158
    subtracting, 157
    Transflectance Channel, 159
    See also MetaPhotos
Angular Pathburst gradient, 58
Angular Shapeburst gradient, 57
animated images, 75, 80–85
    frame transition, 84
    Manual Scooting and, 80
    movie options, 84
    Offspring, 83
    previewing, 84
    recording, 85
    screen size, 84
    See also Interform
Apple Color Wheel, 34
Apply Bubbles, 16
    Apply menu, 44
    arrangement of, 44
    single, 33
    using, 44
    See also Spheroid Designer
Apply modes, 131–135
    Add, 134
    Darken Only, 133

    defined, 131
    Difference, 134
    Lighten Only, 133
    locating, 131
    Multiply, 133
    Normal, 132
    Procedural+, 132
    Procedural-, 132
    Screen, 134
    Subtract, 135
artwork, this book, 5
Auto Resolution dialog box (MetaPhotos), 155
Axis Arrows (Convolver), 140, 146

B

Bump Map panel, 16
    Bump Map menu, 40
    clearing, 33
    illustrated, 40
    See also Spheroid Designer
bump maps
    adding, 40
    adjusting, 41
    choosing, 40–41
    defined, 40
    display, 40
    effect depth, 41
    Golfoid, 40
    height setting, 41
    illustrated sample, 42
    in/out movement, 41
    orientation, 41
    polarity setting, 41
    previewing, 40
    sizing, 41
    See also spheres; Spheroid Designer

C

CD, 8, 11
Channels palette (MetaPhotos), 160

Index

Circular Pathburst gradient, 58
Circular Shapeburst gradient, 57
Circular Sunburst gradient, 55
Clipping Path (MetaPhotos), 160
Color Globe (Texture Explorer 2.1), 111
Color Globe (Texture Explorer), 20, 21
    illustrated, 67
    using, 67
color monitor, 10
Color Picker
    Gradient, 18, 50
    Spheroid Designer, 15
colors (fractals), 123, 124
    inside, 124
    outside, 123
colors (gradient)
    adding, 52
    choosing, 50
    copying, 52
    repeating, 51
colors (spheres), 34
colors (texture)
    changing, 67, 111
    schemes, 67
Compact Filters, 87–97
    3D Stereo Noise, 26, 97
    Apply modes, 131
    defined, 87
    Glass Lens, 26, 88–89
    Glue Control panel, 27
    list of, 87
    Mode Control panel, 27
    Opacity Control panel, 27
    Page Curl, 26, 90–91
    Planar Tile, 26, 92
    Preview window, 27
    Seamless Welder, 26, 93
    Twirl, 26, 94
    Video Feedback, 26, 95
    Vortex Tile, 26, 96
    See also filters
Convolver, 137–151
    Axis Arrows, 140, 146
    Current Tile diamond, 139
    defined, 3
    Design mode, 146

Effect Marbles, 141, 142–147
Effect menu, 140, 146
Effect Names, 140, 146
Explore mode, 140, 147–151
Grid Preview Diamond, 138
    illustrated, 138
    installing, 137–138
    interface, 138–141
    Memory Dots, 149
    Mode buttons, 139
    opening, 141
    Options menu, 150
    Preferences choices, 150
    Preset menu, 149
    Preview window, 148
    Scrubbing, 151
    Stars, 151
    Tweak Difference Mask mode, 146
    Tweak Linear Convolution mode,
        141–144
    Tweak Unsharp/Gaussian mode,
        144–145
    uses, 137
Current Tile diamond (Convolver), 139
Cyclone filter, 12

D

Darken Only Apply mode, 133
Derivative Textures (Texture Explorer 2.1),
    110, 114
Derivative Textures (Texture Explorer), 20, 66
    colors, changing, 67
    defined, 66
    illustrated, 66
    protection, 72
Design mode, 146
    Split Screen Preview, 148
    using, 146
    See also Convolver
Detail Control (Fractal Explorer), 128
Difference Apply mode, 134
Direction Control (Lens f/x), 28
    Edge f/x filter, 102
    Pixel f/x filter, 100
    Smudge f/x filter, 104

Twirl f/x filter, 107
Direction panel (Gradient Designer), 19
    dragging on, 50
    indicator, 50
    Info Area, 49
Direction panel (Texture Explorer), 22, 69
drop shadows, 157

E

Edge f/x filter
    defined, 102
    using, 102
    See also Lens f/x filters
Effect Marbles (Convolver). See marbles
Effect menu (Convolver), 140, 146
Effect Names (Convolver), 140, 146
effects
    Blur, 142
    Brightness, 143
    choosing, 140
    Difference Mask, 146
    direction of, 140
    Edges Amount, 142
    Hue Rotate, 143
    increasing, 141
    intensity of, 144
    mixture of, 146
    names of, 140
    Relief Amount, 143
    Saturation, 143
    Sharpen, 142
    Tint, 144
    See also Convolver
Elliptical Sunburst gradient, 55
Explore mode, 140, 147–151
    Gene Influences menu, 147
    Split Screen Preview, 148
    See also Convolver
Explorer's Guide, 11

F

Father panel
    defined, 24
    illustrated, 23, 24

image types, 76
motion of, 80
See also Interform; Mother panel;
    Offspring panel
File menu (host application)
    Get Info command, 10
    Make Alias command, 9
Filter menu (host application), 8
filters
    3D Stereo Noise, 26, 97
    Compact, 26–27, 87–97
    Cyclone, 12
    Fractal Explorer, 12, 117–129
    Glass Lens, 26, 88–89
    Gradient Designer, 2, 17–19, 47–63
    installing, 9
    Interform, 23–25, 75–85
    KPT 2.1, 12
    KPT 3, 9
    Lens f/x, 28, 99–107
    moving and, 9
    Page Curl, 26, 90–91
    Planar Tile, 26, 92
    Seamless Welder, 26, 93
    Selection Info, 12
    Spheroid Designer, 2, 14–16, 31–35
    Texture Explorer 2.1, 12, 109–115
    Texture Explorer, 20–22, 65–73
    Twirl, 26, 94
    Video Feedback, 26, 95
    Vortex Tile, 26, 96
Fractal Explorer, 12, 117–129
    Apply modes, 131
    clearing, 119
    Color Inside gradient ramp, 119
    Color Outside gradient ramp,
        119, 123, 124
    defined, 117
    Detail Control, 128
    illustrated, 118
    Loop Control, 124
    Map Control panel, 119, 121
    Opacity Control panel, 119, 126
    Preview window, 121, 127
    Repetition Control, 125
    Shuffle button, 127

Spiral Control, 125
starting, 118
Wrapping Controls, 125
Wrapping panel, 123
Zoom Control, 122
Zoom slider, 122
See also filters
fractals
    colors, 123
    defined, 117
    designs, preparing for, 118
    details, 118, 128
    Julia III shape, 120
    Julia II shape, 120
    Julia shape, 120
    looping, 124
    Mandelbrot shape, 120, 121
    M-J Hybrid II shape, 120
    M-J Hybrid I shape, 120
    moving shapes, 121
    naming, 129
    opacity, 126
    overview, 118
    plan, 119
    presets, 129
    repetition, 125
    saving, 129
    spirals, 125
    transparent, 124
    understanding, 118
    zooming in/out of, 122
    See also Fractal Explorer
Frame panels, 25
    filling, 83
    working with, 78
    See also Interform

G

Gaussian f/x filter
    defined, 101
    using, 101
    See also Lens f/x filters
Glass Lens filter, 88–89
    illustrated, 26, 88
    opening, 88

use result, 89
using, 89
See also Compact Filters
Global Controls (Spheroid Designer)
    Ambient Intensity, 36
    defined, 15
    illustrated, 14, 15
    Light Diffusion, 36
    Sphere Curvature, 42
    Transparency, 43
Global Dotes (Spheroid Designer), 14, 15
    Ambient Hue RGB, 34
    Diffuse Hue RGB, 34
glows, 158
Glue Gauge (Lens f/x), 28
Glue Control panel (Compact Filters), 27
Glue Control panel (Gradient Designer), 19
    Normal Apply, 49
    submenu, 49
Glue Control panel (Interform), 25
Glue Control panel (Texture Explorer), 22
Gradient Bar
    defined, 18
    Grayscale Ramp, 53
    illustrated, 18, 50
    Opacity Ramp, 53
    pressing on, 52
    Texture Explorer 2.1, 112, 113
    Texture Explorer, 68
    using, 50
Gradient Bracket, 17, 19
    left "leg," 52
    moving, 52
    resetting, 52
    working with, 52
Gradient Color Picker
    defined, 18
    displaying, 50
    illustrated, 18
Gradient Designer, 2, 17–19, 47–63
    Apply modes, 131
    default settings, 49
    defined, 47
    Direction panel, 19, 49
    elements, 17–19
    Glue Control panel, 19, 49

Gradient Bar, 18, 50, 52–53
Gradient Brackets, 17, 19, 52
Gradient Color Picker, 18
Gradient Modifiers, 18, 61
  illustrated, 17
Loop Control panel, 19, 49
Mode Control panel, 19, 49
Opacity Control panel, 19, 49
Preset Manager, 63
Preset menu, 62, 63
Preview window, 17, 50
Repeat Control panel, 19, 49
settings, clearing, 49
starting, 48
Swap Alpha, 19, 63
Swap RGB, 19, 63
Gradient Modifiers (Gradient Designer)
  adjusting, 61
  Blur, 61
  Brightness, 61
  Contrast, 61
  Cycle, 61
  defined, 18
  Hue, 61
  illustrated, 17, 18
  Saturation, 61
  Squeeze, 61
Gradient Modifiers (Texture Explorer)
  adjusting, 71
  Blur, 71
  Brightness, 71
  Contrast, 71
  Cycle, 71
  defined, 21
  Hue, 71
  illustrated, 20, 21
  Saturation, 71
  Squeeze, 71
gradients, 47–63
  angle of, 50
  Angular Shapeburst, 57
  blending rate, 60
  blurring, 61
  brightness, 61
  center, changing, 57
  choosing colors for, 50

  Circular Shapeburst, 57
  Circular Sunbursts, 55
  colors, 50–52
  contrast, 61
  creation preparation, 48
  defined, 47
  direction, 50
  Elliptical Sunburst, 55
  Grayscale Mapburst, 59
  gray shades, 53
  hue, 61
  loop, 50
  opacity, 54
  order of, 60
  preset, 62
  Radial Sweep, 56
  Rectangular Burst, 56
  repetitions, 51
  saturation, 61
  Square Burst, 56
  squeezing, 61
  three-color, 48, 51
  transparency, 53
Gradient Strip (Texture Explorer), 20, 21
Grayscale Mapburst, 59
Grid Preview Diamond
  effect direction, 140
  illustrated, 139
  See also Convolver

H

Help button, 29
HiRes files, 154
  sizes, changing, 154–155
  See also MetaPhotos
host applications, 7
  defined, 7
  Filter menu, 8
  Get Info window, 10
  plug-ins folder, 8, 9
  RAM allocation to, 10–11
  types of, 7

I

images
    animated, 75, 80–85
    blending, 82
    composite, 156
    opacity, 79
    recording, 85
    static, 75, 76–79
Image Size dialog box (MetaPhotos), 154
installation, 7–12
    with alias, 9
    CD, 8
    Convolver, 137–138
    host applications and, 7
    Kai's Classic Power Tips, 11–12
    KPT 2.1 filters, 12
    KPT 3 filters, 9
    KPT Actions, 162
    process, 8
    registration, 9
    system requirements, 10
    tips, 9
Intensity Control (Lens f/x), 28
    Edge f/x filter, 102
    Gaussian f/x filter, 101
    Intensity f/x filter, 103
    Noise f/x filter, 105
    Pixel f/x filter, 100
    Smudge f/x filter, 104
    Twirl f/x filter, 107
Intensity f/x filter
    defined, 103
    using, 103
    See also Lens f/x filters
interface, 13–29
    Compact Filters, 26–27
    Convolver, 138–141
    Gradient Designer, 17–19
    Interform, 23–25
    Lens f/x, 28–29
    Spheroid Designer, 14–16
    Texture Explorer, 20–22
Interform, 23–25, 75–85
    Add Presets button, 78
    Apply modes, 131
    Blending triangle, 82
    elements, 23–25
    Father panel, 23, 24, 76, 80
    Frame panels, 25, 78, 83
    Glue Control panel, 25
    illustrated, 23
    Manual Blending, 82
    Manual Scooting, 80
    Mother panel, 23, 24, 76
    motion options, turning off, 76
    Motion Triangles, 23, 24
    Movie Options, 84
    Offspring panel, 23, 24, 76
    Opacity Control panel, 25, 79
    Preset menu, 79
    Record Keyframes button,
        23, 25, 85
    starting, 76
    UniMotion Options, 23, 24, 81
    See also filters

K

Kai logo, 29
Kai's Classic Power Tips, 11–12
    defined, 11
    folder, 11
    installation, 11–12
Kai's Power Tips, 1
Kai's Power Tools
    history of, 1–2
    installation, 7–12
    interest in, 2
Kaleidoscope filter, 94
KPT 3 Manual, 11
KPT Actions, 161–169
    Actions palette, 163, 167
    Backgrounds, 165
    buttons, 165
    categories of, 164
    defined, 4, 161
    Delete Action button, 168
    Effects Perplexer, 168–169
    finding, 162
    folder, 162
    Frame, 164

installing, 162
loading, 162
modifying, 168–169
New Action button, 166, 168
Opacity Control panel, 169
Play button, 163
presets, 162, 166
recording, 166–167
requirements, 161
running, 163–166
Stop Recording button, 167
Text, 164
KPT Texture Explorer, 2
Krause, Kai, 1, 126

L

Lamp Controls, 15
Highlight Intensity, 36
Light Hue in RGB, 34
Light Intensity, 36
Light Polarity, 33, 37
See also Spheroid Designer
Lamps
changing direction of, 35, 37
defined, 14
illustrated, 14
multiple, 37
turned on/off, 33
See also Spheroid Designer
lens
circular, 88
elliptical, 88
illustrated, 89
lighting, 89
opacity, 89
Lens f/x filters, 28, 99–107
Apply modes, 131
Edge f/x, 102
elements, 28
Gaussian f/x, 101
Intensity f/x, 103
interface, 28, 99
list of, 99
Metatoys f/x, 106
moving, 99

Noise f/x, 105
Pixel f/x, 100
previews and, 99
Smudge f/x, 104
Twirl f/x, 107
See also filters
Lighten Only Apply mode, 133
lighting
lens, 89
spheres, 35
Loop Control panel, 19
adjusting, 60
effects, 60
No Distortion, 49, 60
Pinch Inward, 60
Pinch Left, 60
Pinch Outward, 60
Pinch Right, 60
Sawtooth A->B, 49, 60
Sawtooth B->A, 60
submenu, 49
Triangle A->B->A, 60
Triangle B->A->B, 60
See also Gradient Designer
LoRes files, 154

M

manuals
electronic, 11
Explorer's Guide, 11
Map panel (Fractal Explorer), 119, 121
marbles
Blur, 142
Brightness, 143
Color Control, 144
Edges Amount, 142, 143
Edges Angle, 142
Effect Intensity, 144
Fade to Grey, 144
Gaussian, 144, 145
Gene Influence, 147
Genetic Diversity, 147
Hue Rotate, 143
Mutate Genes, 147
Radius, 144, 145

Reset to Normal, 141, 144
Saturation, 143
Sharpen, 142
Threshold, 144, 145
Tint, 144
Unsharp, 144, 145
See also Convolver
matte surfaces, 36
Memory Dots (Convolver), 149
Memory Dots (Spheroid Designer), 16
clearing, 38
gold, 38
illustrated, 38
MetaPhotos, 153–160
Alpha Channels, 156–159
Auto Resolution dialog box, 155
Channels palette, 160
Clipping Path dialog box, 160
collections, 4
defined, 3–4
HiRes, 154
Image Size dialog box, 154
LoRes, 154
obtaining, 153
Paths palette, 160
Save Path dialog box (MetaPhotos),
160
Transflectance Channel, 159
MetaTools, 9
Metatoys f/x filter
defined, 106
Kaleida mode, 107
using, 106
See also Lens f/x filters
Mode Gauge (Lens f/x), 28
Edge f/x filter, 102
Gaussian f/x filter, 101
Metatoys f/x filter, 106
Noise f/x filter, 105
Pixel f/x filter, 100
Smudge f/x filter, 104
Twirl f/x filter, 107
Mode Control panel (Compact Filters), 27
3D Stereo Noise filter, 97
Page Curl filter, 90
Planar Tile filter, 92

Seamless Welder filter, 93
Twirl filter, 94
Video Feedback filter, 95
Vortex Tile filter, 96
Mode Control panel (Gradient Designer), 19
Angular Pathburst, 58
Angular Shapeburst, 57
Circular Pathburst, 58
Circular Shapeburst, 57
Circular Sunburst, 55
Elliptical Sunburst, 55
Gradients on Paths, 58
Grayscale Mapburst, 59
Linear Blend, 49
Radial Sweep, 56
Rectangular Burst, 56
Square Burst, 56
submenu, 49
Mother panel
defined, 24
illustrated, 23, 24
image types, 76
motion of, 80
See also Father panel; Interform;
Offspring panel
Motion Triangles (Interform), 24
Movie Options (Interform), 84
movies
frame transitions, 84
previewing, 84
recording, 85
saving, 85
screen size, 84
See also Interform
Multiply Apply mode, 133
mutations
controlling (Texture
Explorer 2.1), 110
options, 67
sphere, 45
texture, 66–67
Mutation Tree (Spheroid Designer), 45
defined, 15
illustrated, 14, 15
options, 45
using, 45

Mutation Tree (Texture Explorer 2.1), 110, 111
Mutation Tree (Texture Explorer), 20, 21
    colors, 66
    defined, 21
    illustrated, 66
    Mutation Options menu, 67

N

Noise f/x filter
    defined, 105
    using, 105
    See also Lens f/x filters
Normal Apply mode, 132

O

Offspring panel
    blending, 82
    defined, 24
    illustrated, 23, 24
    image types, 76
    motion of, 80
    See also Father panel; Interform;
        Mother panel
opacity
    action, 169
    fractals, 126
    gradient, 54
    image, 79
    lens, 89
    page curl, 91
    texture, 70
    vortex tile, 96
Opacity Control (Lens f/x), 28
    Edge f/x filter, 102
    Gaussian f/x filter, 101
    Intensity f/x filter, 103
    Metatoys f/x filter, 106
    Noise f/x filter, 105
    Pixel f/x filter, 100
    Smudge f/x filter, 104
    Twirl f/x filter, 107
Opacity Control panel (Compact Filters), 27
    3D Stereo Noise filter, 97
    Glass Lens filter, 89

Page Curl filter, 91
Planar Tile filter, 92
Seamless Welder filter, 93
Video Feedback filter, 95
Vortex Tile filter, 96
Opacity Control panel (Fractal Explorer), 119
    Opacity menu, 126
    settings, 126
    using, 126
Opacity Control panel (Gradient Designer), 19
    dragging, 54
    submenu, 49
    using, 54
Opacity Control panel (Interform), 25
    dragging in, 79
    using, 79
Opacity Control panel (KPT Actions), 169
Opacity Control panel (Texture Explorer), 22
    dragging in, 70
    using, 70
Options Gauge (Lens f/x), 28
    Metatoys f/x filter, 106
    Noise f/x filter, 105
    Smudge f/x filter, 104

P

Page Curl filter, 90–91
    illustrated, 26, 90
    opening, 90
    See also Compact Filters
page curls
    color, 90
    direction, 90
    illustrated, 91
    multiple, 91
    opacity, 91
    transparent, 91
Paths palette (MetaPhotos), 160
Photoshop, 1–2, 7
    Kai's Classic Power Tips and, 11–12
    Plug-ins folder, 8
Pixel f/x filter
    defined, 100
    using, 100
    See also Lens f/x filters

Planar Tile filter, 92
    illustrated, 26
    starting, 92
    using, 92
    See also Compact Filters
plug-ins folder, 9
PowerPhotos. See MetaPhotos
Preset Manager (Gradient Designer), 63
Preset menu
    Fractal Explorer, 129
    Gradient Designer, 62, 63
    Interform, 79
    keyboard shortcuts, 115
    Spheroid Designer, 39
    Texture Explorer 2.1, 115
    Texture Explorer, 72–73
presets
    adding, 29, 38, 62, 72, 78
    applying, 73
    deleting, 29
    fractals, 129
    KPT Actions, 162, 166
    loading, 149
    naming, 38, 62, 72, 78, 149
    preferences, 39, 73
    selecting, 39, 62, 73, 79
previews
    animation, 84
    bump map, 40
    Lens f/x filters and, 99
    spheres, 33, 43
    See also Preview windows
Preview Sphere, 14
    changing light direction with, 35
    defined, 14
    See also Spheroid Designer
Preview windows
    Compact Filters, 27, 89–97
    Convolver, 148
    Fractal Explorer, 121, 127
    Gradient Designer, 17, 50, 54
    Lens f/x filter, 100–107
    Texture Explorer 2.1, 110, 112, 113
    Texture Explorer, 66, 67, 69
Procedural+ Apply mode, 132
Procedural- Apply mode, 132

Q

QuickTime, 75
    Compression Settings dialog box, 85
    format, 85

R

Radial Sweep gradient, 56
RAM, increasing, 10–11
Record Keyframes button (Interform), 25, 85
Rectangular Burst gradient, 56
registration, 9
Repeat panel, 19
    clicking in, 51
    dragging in, 51
    Info Area, 49
    See also Gradient Designer
Repetition Control (Fractal Explorer), 125
Reset button (Lens f/x), 28

S

Save Path dialog box (MetaPhotos), 160
Screen Apply mode, 134
Seamless Welder filter, 93
    illustrated, 26
    opening, 93
    using, 93
    See also Compact Filters
Shuffle button (Fractal Explorer), 127
Smudge f/x filter
    defined, 104
    using, 104
    See also Lens f/x filter
Source Texture (Texture Explorer 2.1)
    changing, 110
    moving, 112
Source Texture (Texture Explorer), 20, 66
    derivatives, 68
    dragging, 68
    establishing, 67
    moving, 68
spheres
    arrangement of, 44
    bump maps, 40–41

coloring, 34–35
color swirls on, 37
creation preparation, 32–33
curvature of, 42
file height/width of, 32
full screen preview of, 33
on layers, 32
lighting, 35
matte surfaces, 36
multiple, 44
multiple lamps on, 37
one lamp on, 33
shiny surfaces, 36
transparency of, 43
Spheroid Designer, 2, 14–16, 31–45
Add Preset button, 38
Apply Bubbles, 16
Apply modes, 131
Bump Map panel, 16
clearing settings, 33
Color Picker, 15
default settings, 33
elements, 14–16
Global Controls, 15
illustrated, 14
Lamp Controls, 15
Lamps, 14
Memory Dots Grid, 16, 38
Mutation Tree, 15
Preset menu, 39
Preview Sphere, 14
settings, saving, 38
Small Bump Dots, 16
Small Global Dots, 15
starting, 32
See also filters; spheres
Spiral Control (Fractal Explorer), 125
Square Burst gradient, 56
Stars (Convolver), 151
static images, 75
Subtract Apply mode, 135
Swap RGB/Alpha, 17, 19, 63
system requirements, 10

T

TE & FE Classic folder, 12
Texture Explorer 2.1, 12, 109–115
Add Preset button, 115
Apply modes, 131
Color Globe, 111
Derivative Texture, 110, 114
differences in, 109
Gradient Bar, 112
Mutation Tree, 110
Preset menu, 115
Preview window, 110, 112, 113
Shuffle button, 111
Source Texture, 110, 112
starting, 110
Texture Protection, 114
Transparency Option, 113
See also filters
Texture Explorer, 20–22, 65–73
Apply modes, 131
Color Globe, 21
defined, 65
Derivative Textures, 20, 66
Direction Control panel, 22
elements, 20–22
Glue Control panel, 22
Gradient Bar, 68
Gradient Modifiers, 21, 71
Gradient Strip, 21
illustrated, 20
Mutation Tree, 21
Opacity Control panel, 22, 70
Preset menu, 72–73
Source Texture, 20, 66, 67, 68
starting, 65
See also filters
textures (Interform)
blending, 82
creation preparation, 76
Offspring, 77
Parent, 77, 82
textures (Texture Explorer 2.1)
creation preparation, 110
presets and, 109
repeating, 109

textures, 65–73
   blurring, 71
   brightness, 71
   colors, 67
   contrast, 71
   creation preparation, 65
   direction of, 69
   hue, 71
   mutations, 66–67
   opacity, 70
   protection, setting, 72, 114
   saturation, 71
   saving, 72–73
   size, changing, 69
   squeezing, 71
Transflectance Channels, 159
transparency
   fractal, 124
   gradient, 53
   page curl, 91
   sphere, 43
   texture, 113
Tweak mode
   clearing, 141
   Difference Mask, 146
   Linear Convolution, 141–144
   Unsharp/Gaussian, 144–145
   See also Convolver
Twirl filter, 94
   illustrated, 26
   Kaleidoscope mode, 94
   opening, 94
   Twirl mode, 94
   See also Compact Filters
Twirl f/x filter
   Kaleida mode, 107
   using, 107
   See also Lens f/x filter

U

UniMotion Options, 24
   displaying, 80
   Manual Blending, 82
   Manual Scooting, 80
   menu, 80
   speed, changing, 81
   using, 81
   See also Interform

V

Video Feedback filter, 95
   Feedback Intensity Control, 95
   illustrated, 26
   opening, 95
   Telescopic Feedback mode, 95
   using, 95
   See also Compact Filters
Vortex Tile filter, 96
   illustrated, 26
   opening, 96
   using, 96
   See also Compact Filters

W

Wilczak, John, 1
Wrapping Controls (Fractal Explorer), 125
Wrapping panel (Fractal Explorer), 123

Z

Zoom slider (Fractal Explorer), 122